BOXING IN THE LOS ANGELES AREA 1880-2005

BY

TRACY CALLIS
CHUCK JOHNSTON

Trafford Publishing

Order this book online at www.trafford.com
or email orders@trafford.com

Most Trafford titles are also available at major online book retailers.

Printed in Victoria, BC, Canada.

ISBN: 978-1-4269-1688-5 (Soft)

*Our mission is to efficiently provide the world's finest, most comprehensive
book publishing service, enabling every author to experience success.
To find out how to publish your book, your way, and have it available
worldwide, visit us online at www.trafford.com*

Trafford rev. 11/10/2009

 www.trafford.com

North America & international
toll-free: 1 888 232 4444 (USA & Canada)
phone: 250 383 6864 ♦ fax: 812 355 4082

TABLE OF CONTENTS

Acknowledgements

The authors offer a special thank you to all those who contributed to the development of this book, for assistance in various ways and for photographs provided --

Joe Cardoza Jr.
Doug Cavanaugh
Chicago Historical Society
Tom Hogan, Hogan Photos, Los Angeles, California
Bruce Jarvis
J.J. Johnston
Los Angeles Public Library (Herald-Examiner Collection, Security Pacific Collection)
Clay Moyle (www.prizefightingbooks.com)
Gabriel "Hap" Navarro
Lupe Ortiz Saldana
Jan Sanders, Los Angeles, California
Tom Scharf
William Schutte
Richard Self
Harry and Raven Shaffer (Antiquities of the Prize Ring; www.antekprizering.com)
Jerome Shochet
Kevin Smith
Daaave Summers
Bruce Torrence, www.HollywoodPhotographs.com
U.C.L.A. (Special Collections)
University of Southern California

The authors also offer a great thank you to our families for their patience and understanding during the writing of this book – From Tracy Callis to Barbara Callis, wife; Tracy Jr., Jonas and Seth, sons; From Chuck Johnston to his family

Introduction

The huge metropolis of Los Angeles, California has been one of the great pugilistic hotbeds in the world, having had almost continuous boxing activity since the 1880s. More than any other boxing site in the United States, Los Angeles continues to have a vibrant boxing culture with its large number of fans, boxers, and boxing men - promoters, managers, matchmakers and trainers.

Largely a white boxing culture at the beginning, it became dominated by people of Mexican descent in the second half of the Twentieth Century.

The Los Angeles ascent to being one of the premier boxing cities is directly linked to its location and the history of boxing in California. During the second half of the 1800s, California was a boxing center due to the fact that San Francisco, the biggest and most important city in California by a huge margin at the time, was one of the greatest boxing cities of the world.

In the 1880s and 1890s, the much smaller Los Angeles had only small, short-lived boxing clubs staging minor bouts. By 1901, professional boxing became highly restricted or illegal in many states, notably in New York and Illinois. As a result, California had more important bouts than any other state from 1901 to 1914.

It was in 1901 that Tom McCarey staged boxing cards witnessed by good-sized crowds at Hazard's Pavilion, putting Los Angeles on the map as a major boxing location. McCarey went on to stage many important bouts at the Pacific Athletic Club Pavilion in the Naud Junction area of downtown Los Angeles and then at an open-air arena in the nearby small town of Vernon.

In the November 1914 election, a majority of California voters cast their ballots in favor of an amendment that limited boxing bouts to a maximum of four rounds with the largest value of a prize set at $25. This was enacted with the intent of banning professional boxing in California. As a result of the new law, boxing cards with only four-round bouts were staged at boxing clubs throughout California from late 1914 to the beginning of 1925.

During this period, Jack Doyle was the premier promoter in the Los Angeles area, staging weekly boxing cards with a great deal of success in Vernon. As boxing became more popular during the early 1920s, there were weekly boxing cards staged at a large number of new venues in the Los Angeles area, which included the venerable Hollywood Legion Stadium, the Wilmington Bowl, the Chief Petty Officers Club in San Pedro, the Armory in Pasadena and the Lyceum in Los Angeles.

During the November 1924 election, a majority of California voters cast their ballots in favor of an amendment that permitted bouts scheduled for a maximum of ten rounds if there was a decision or for a maximum of twelve rounds if there was no decision. The new law also had a provision establishing a state athletic commission that had control of professional boxing, professional wrestling and some amateur boxing cards in California.

Due to the fact that Los Angeles had much boxing activity over the years, there were a large number of top boxers who lived in the vicinity. They included Solomon "Solly" Smith, Jim Jeffries, "Mexican" Joe Rivers, Bert Colima, Fidel LaBarba, Jimmy McLarnin, Ace Hudkins, Jackie Fields, Newsboy Brown, Speedy Dado, Alberto "Baby" Arizmendi, Henry Armstrong, Enrique Bolanos, Art Aragon, Jerry Quarry, Armando "Mando" Ramos, Armando Muniz, Danny "Little Red" Lopez, Bobby Chacon, Oscar De La Hoya and "Sugar" Shane Mosley.

Many of the top boxing people were based in Los Angeles too. They included Tom McCarey, Jack Doyle, Hayden "Wad" Wadhams, Joe Levy, Pop Foster, Tom Gallery, Clyde Hudkins, Charley MacDonald, Morrie Cohen, Joe Waterman, George Parnassus, "Babe" McCoy (Harry Rudolph McCoy), Cal Eaton, Aileen Eaton, Jackie McCoy, Howie Steindler, Mickey Davies, Don Chargin, John Jackson and Antonio Curtis. Among the noted Los Angeles ring announcers were Dan Tobey, Jimmy Lennon and Jimmy Lennon, Jr.

Over the years, there were many famous boxing venues and gyms in the Los Angeles area. Among these, not already mentioned were the Los Angeles Athletic Club, the Jeffries Athletic Club (an open-air arena), the Olympic Auditorium, Wrigley Field, Gilmore Stadium, Ocean Park Arena (at least two versions), Eastside Arena, the Sports Arena, the Coliseum, the Forum and the Staples Center. The famed Los Angeles-based gyms included the Manhattan, the Main Street Gym and the Hoover Street Gym.

WORKING OUT IN THE GYM. A group of Los Angeles boxing hopefuls took time out and posed for a picture in the Manhattan Gym in Los Angeles (circa 1946). Left to right they are Chuck Cruz, Dave Loiga, Kobie Scott, Leo Flores, Al Medrano, Silver Rodriguez and Johnny Murray.

Chapter One

The Early Years

1880-1900

From 1880 to 1900, Los Angeles was a relatively small city located in a sparsely populated area known as Southern California. During the same period, San Francisco, located in the more populated area called Northern California, was the major city in California in every respect. It was also one of the most important boxing centers in the world under both the London Prize Ring and the Marquis of Queensberry Rules.

The following population table gives a good indication of the importance of San Francisco as compared to Los Angeles during the late Nineteenth Century:

Population Table

Year	Los Angeles	San Francisco	California
1880	11,183	233,959	864,694
1890	50,395	298,997	1,213,398
1900	102,479	342,782	1,485,053

Sources: Los Angeles Almanac; www.zpub.com

The data shows that the population of Los Angeles grew at a very rapid pace. In fact, Los Angeles became one of the major cities in the United States within the first two or three decades of the Twentieth Century.

Due to its large working class population at the time, San Francisco was blessed with a large boxing fan base. Many top boxers were born in the city during these early years and a number of excellent fighters came from Australia and New Zealand. Since San Francisco was the major seaport on the West Coast of the United States, a good many of the foreign boxers had their first bouts on American soil in that city. Top boxers from just about all parts of the United States traveled to San Francisco to get bouts against the better fighters.

During this time in Los Angeles, there were some short-lived, small athletic clubs. A number of them were located in the Downey Block area, staging minor bouts in clubrooms witnessed by small crowds. There were relatively few boxing cards staged during a given year.

Of all the athletic clubs in the area, the Los Angeles Athletic Club (LAAC) was the best known. It was founded in 1880 and exists to the present day. The LAAC provided athletic facilities for use by its members and staged various athletic events, including boxing contests and tournaments. The LAAC was to become the owner of the Olympic Auditorium, a site that was the most famous boxing venue in Los Angeles for many decades. As a result, the LAAC played a major role in the amateur and professional boxing history of the Los Angeles area.

Frank Garbutt, a prominent Los Angeles business man, was influential in the development of the Los Angeles Athletic Club. Garbutt was also a central figure in a number of important boxing events in Los Angeles during the first half of the Twentieth Century, many of which pertained to the Olympic Auditorium.

The LAAC hired a number of boxing instructors who were heavily involved in local boxing. One talented instructor and noted professional boxer was Billy Gallagher. He also managed a young heavyweight, Jim Jeffries, who was a member of the LAAC at the beginning of the latter's great career.

Another instructor of the era was DeWitt Van Court, who lived in the San Francisco boxing hotbed before coming to Los Angeles. As a result, he knew many of the boxing people of that day. Van Court wrote a number of articles about boxing for the Los Angeles Times over the decades in addition to a small book that was published during the 1920s.

The LAAC staged a number of professional boxing cards during the 1880-1900 period. It was difficult to line up long distance bouts at times, so the club provided shows (or smokers) featuring different kinds of entertainment. The shows included short boxing and wrestling bouts (or exhibitions), musical programs and even storytelling. After 1900, the LAAC ceased staging professional boxing bouts.

In these early years, most of the boxing cards featured a main event and several preliminary bouts. At first, a main event was a fight-to-a-finish contest. By the middle 1890s, it was scheduled for a fixed number of rounds and by the late 1890s, main events usually were scheduled for twenty rounds.

Preliminary bouts were generally short in duration, most scheduled for four rounds. At first, none of these results were listed in the newspapers. During the late 1890s, there were cards in which preliminary bouts were longer in duration and these decisions were listed in the newspapers.

Despite the relatively small size of the boxing clubs in Los Angeles and the lack of boxing activity at this time, there were some top boxers who were from the area. A native of Los Angeles named Solomon "Solly" Smith was the first boxer from Southern California to win a world title. He captured the World Featherweight Championship from George Dixon in San Francisco on October 4, 1897.

Jim Jeffries, a native of Ohio who moved to the Los Angeles area as a child in the early 1880s, was a huge man for the time, standing nearly 6'3" in height and weighing a hard 220 pounds in prime condition. Besides being an exceptionally strong and durable hard puncher, he was considered to be a very good, quick all-around athlete.

On June 9, 1899, Jeffries won the World Heavyweight Championship from Bob Fitzsimmons at Coney Island in New York. Jeffries defended his title seven times during his reign before retiring undefeated in 1905. For much of the Twentieth Century, many people regarded Jeffries as the best heavyweight boxer of all time.

Both Smith and Jeffries traveled to other parts of the country for most of their respective bouts. Smith did have a number of verified bouts in the Los Angeles area during the early years and late years of his career. Jeffries had only one, a bout with Joe Goddard at Hazard's Pavilion in 1898.

During the 1880s and 1890s, many of the professional boxers who fought on boxing cards in Los Angeles lived in the area. However, it appears that a number of these boxers moved to other parts of the country a short time later because of the greater boxing activity there. In addition to Smith, Gallagher and Jeffries, other boxers who lived in Los Angeles for at least a short time during this period included Billy Manning, Frank Childs, Gus Hergett, Harry Peppers, "Utah" Bob Thompson, Fred Bogan, Hank Griffin, Joe Soto, Kid Williams (whose real name was Frank or Charles Solomon), Rufus Thompson and the Dixie Kid (Aaron Brown).

THE BEGINNING. On the evening of September 8, 1880, the Los Angeles Athletic Club (LAAC) was established in the old Arcadia building located on North Spring Street. Forty citizens gathered in Frank Gibson's law office, on the second floor of the old McDonald Block on Main Street, to create the new club. During the 1880-1900 years, the club became a center of activity for residents of Los Angeles who were interested in health and recreation. Monthly dues were set at $1. The initiation fee was $5. Ladies were welcome at social events and exhibitions. Colonel James B. Lankershim, whose family owned a good portion of the San Fernando Valley, was elected as the first LAAC president. **(Courtesy UCLA Special Collections)**

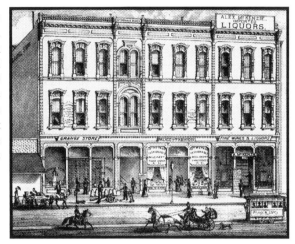

LOS ANGELES ATHLETIC CLUB GYM. Club members stayed busy exercising in the gym. LAAC members excelled at gymnastics, boxing, handball and velocipede (tall bicycle) racing. Gym equipment consisted largely of a trapeze, flying rings, long horse, Indian clubs and dumbbells. **(Courtesy UCLA Special Collections)**

SECOND HOME. From 1882 to 1889, the Downey Block was home of the LAAC. Rooms were renovated in the main building for use by club members. A gymnasium was constructed at the rear, on New High Street (visible as a black peaked roof with skylights, center right). Over the years, the club's membership consisted of many outstanding members of Los Angeles. A number of the members were prominent in the changes and developments of the city since its beginning as a small town. **(Courtesy UCLA Special Collections)**

UP AND COMING. Billy Manning, an up and coming fighter who appeared in Los Angeles on a regular basis, took the measure of Tom Palmer in seven rounds on March 7, 1885 at the original Turnverein Hall. The contest was fought with gloves and watched closely by authorities so that it did not get out of hand. Neither man was battered nor bloody but Palmer did suffer an arm injury that brought an end to the contest.

With Soft Gloves.

Turnverein Hall was jammed last night by spectators, attracted by the glove-contest to a finish between Billy Manning and Tom Palmer. In preliminary set-tos by local talent, DeGrasse "bested" Costello; Devere and McCoy fought a draw; and Jones did up Daly. For the wind-up between Manning and Palmer, Thos. Madden was referee. The rivals were in fine trim and gave a good exhibition of scientific sparring. Police were present to check any brutality, but their services were not needed. The contest was spirited, but there were neither blood nor knock-downs. In the seventh round, Palmer, who was in the lead, sprained his right arm beyond use, and the match went to Manning.

A GREAT ONE. During 1885, Jack Dempsey, the "Nonpareil," toured California giving boxing exhibitions and taking on all-comers. Dempsey won many of his California fights by knockout. Billy Manning, of Los Angeles, tangled with the great fighter on August 29, 1885 at Turnverein Hall and was stopped in seven rounds. Manning was muscular, feisty and tough but was completely outclassed by the fancy Dempsey. Billy finally succumbed to the slick moving and skillful hitting Dempsey, who bloodied him up and knocked him down several times before stopping him. (An early book on Dempsey, by Richard Fox, claimed the fight was held at Turn Hall in San Francisco.)

THE IRISH TRAVELER. Jack Burke, the "Irish Lad," visited Los Angeles on October 15, 1886 and knocked out Jim Carr in three rounds. Burke traveled the world over during his career that spanned from 1878 to 1894 and exhibited his skills for boxing fans in England, America, Australia, New Zealand and South Africa. He fought such outstanding men of his day as John L. Sullivan, Jim Corbett, Peter Jackson, "Nonpareil" Jack Dempsey, Frank "Paddy" Slavin, Jake Kilrain, Charlie Mitchell, Alf Greenfield, Mike Cleary, Larry Foley and Frank Glover. **(Courtesy Antiquities of the Prize Ring)**

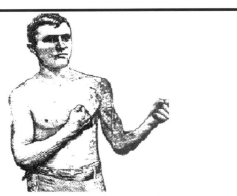

Dempsey did up Jones in three rounds at the hard-glove contest at Billy Manning's last night - April 18, 1885

CALIFORNIA JACK. The Golden State had its own version of Jack Dempsey in a lightweight of that name. This Dempsey fought primarily in California during 1884-1891. Circa 1886, he knocked out Billy Devere in one round in Los Angeles. Jack also claimed wins over Harry Jones, George Van Pool, Frank Nevitt, Young Moran, Tom Stockley and Jack Davis during his ring career.

PACIFIC COAST CHAMPION. Tommy Warren was born in Los Angeles but never boxed an official contest here. Warren was a prominent fighter of his day and the Featherweight Champion of the Pacific Coast during the mid-1880s. He also claimed to be Featherweight Champion of America during the 1880s. His career lasted from the early 1880s until 1900. During this time, he defeated such men as Bob Haight, Johnny Keating, Andy Hanley, Arthur Majesty, Tommy Barnes, Patsy Cahill, Tommy Danforth, Patsy O'Leary, George Siddons, Johnny Murphy, John Van Heest, Jack Havlin and Tommy Miller. (**Courtesy Antiquties of the Prize Ring**)

A PAVILION.

Huge Structure to be Built on Fifth and Olive.

Kysor & Morgan, the architects, have in their office completed plans of a large pavilion, to be erected on the corner of Fifth and Olive streets, opposite the Sixth Street Park. The land is owned by Hon. H. T. Hazard, and he will have associated with him in the ownership of the building H. K. S. O'Melveny and Col. C. H. Howland. It was originally intended to have the pavilion ready for the Republican State Convention which met here in August, but the absence of Mr. Hazard in Sacramento necessitated a postponement.

THE PLAN. Here is a newspaper clipping from the Los Angeles Times, dated October 22, 1886, that discusses the plan for the new Pavilion to be built on the corner of Fifth and Olive Streets. The land selected belonged to Henry T. Hazard and the building was eventually named after him.

A PROGRESSIVE MAN. Henry Thomas Hazard was a charter member of the Los Angeles Bar Association and was fundamental in the construction of the Pavilion named after him. He was born in Grosse Point, Michigan in 1844 and came to Los Angeles as a youth in 1853. As an adult, he became a lawyer, advanced to the position of City Attorney, served as Mayor from 1889 to 1892 and eventually became a state legislator. **(Courtesy SECURITY PACIFIC COLLECTION / Los Angeles Public Library)**

HAZARD'S PAVILION. The famous Hazard Pavilion was built during 1887. It was the largest auditorium in Southern California and seated 4,000, including a restaurant and art salon. It had square cupola-topped towers flanking the main entrance and a 50 foot ceiling. The Pavilion was a cultural center for various social activities including music, dance, theatre and opera. It became the venue where Tom McCarey, the great boxing promoter in Los Angeles, staged his first shows. As a result, it was sometimes said that Hazard's Pavilion was the "cradle of big-time boxing in Los Angeles." The building was torn down around 1906 to make way for another landmark, the Philharmonic Auditorium (McClune's Auditorium). **(Courtesy SECURITY PACIFIC COLLECTION / Los Angeles Public Library)**

A DETERMINED FELLOW. On May 24, 1887, Billy Manning signed articles of agreement to fight Tom Cleary, of San Francisco, once again. He had tangled with Cleary twice before, in 1884, and lost both times in rugged battles. This third fight between the two men was held in June, near Los Angeles, and ended in a ten round draw.

Several Glove-fighters Anxious for Gore—Maybe.

The following articles of agreement between Cleary and Manning were signed yesterday:

Los ANGELES, May 24, 1887.

We, the undersigned, Tom Cleary, of San Francisco, and Billy Manning, of Los Angeles, hereby agree to meet and fight to a finish, with skin gloves, for a purse of $500.

The fight to take place within two weeks, within fifty miles of Los Angeles. The winner to take $300 and the loser $200. No money to be paid to either party unless a committee of three, to be selected by the referee from the audience, will decide that the fight is a good, square and genuine fight. Signed in presence of J. J. Donovan.

BILLY MANNING.

TOM CLEARY.

NEW TURNVEREIN HALL. This is a photo of the new Turnverein Hall Building in 1888, located at 321 South Main Street. The group posing in front was a club of German Americans. Many social and athletic events, including boxing, were held there. **(Courtesy SECURITY PACIFIC COLLECTION / Los Angeles Public Library)**

SCRAPPY LITTLE GUY. Solomon Garcia Smith, better known as "Solly" Smith, had a long and successful career beginning around 1888 and lasting until 1904. He fought often in Los Angeles during his early years. By the time he finished fighting, he had defeated such men as George Dixon, "Torpedo" Billy Murphy, Dennis Mahoney, Dal Hawkins, Dan Daly, John Van Heest, Johnny Griffin, Oscar Gardner, Martin Flaherty, Frank Patterson and Billy Maynard. **(Courtesy Tom Scharf)**

A BIG PURSE DEPOSITED

For the Battle Between Jack Dempsey and Joe Ellingsworth.

A message was received in this city yesterday from Los Angeles, Cal., stating that the managers of the Southern California Athletic Club had deposited a purse of $3,000 at that place for the coming fight between Jack Dempsey, of Brooklyn, the middle weight champion, and Joe Ellingsworth, of New York. The battle will be for the championship. Both men are now at Los Angeles, and are to go into training under the eye of the Athletic Club managers. The fight will probably be fixed for July 4 at Los Angeles. Ellingsworth has been anxious to get at Dempsey ever since he last won the amateur middle weight championship.

LOOKS LIKE A BIG FIGHT COMING UP. Here is a Los Angeles Times clipping (May 18, 1889) that speaks of an effort by the Southern California Athletic Club (SCAC) to bring together "Nonpareil" Jack Dempsey and Joe Ellingsworth in a middleweight boxing contest. Ellingsworth had been after a fight with Dempsey for several years and now had the backing of the SCAC. However, the bout never materialized.

'FRISCO FIGHTER. Joe Soto (called Joe De Soto in the article to the right) was a prominent featherweight from the San Francisco area. He ventured south to Los Angeles on May 21, 1889 and knocked out Harry Jones in 21 rounds at the Los Angeles Athletic Club. On September 26, 1889, he was back in town and fought durable Tommy Danforth, who was a former Featherweight Champion of New York. Soto won after fifty-five rounds.

Dal Hawkins   Fred Bogan

HAWKINS & BOGAN

A REAL BOXING MAN. Fred Bogan (on the right) is seen with Dal Hawkins. They met in the ring on three official occasions. One contest was a marathon venture that required something like 85 to 91 rounds (reports vary) and two days to complete. Fred was involved in many endeavors related to boxing during his life. He boxed from 1887 until 1900 and had a sparkling record that included the National Amateur and Pacific Coast Featherweight Championships. After his fighting days were finished, he wrote articles for a newspaper, ran some bath houses, was proprietor of a hotel, promoted boxing matches, refereed bouts, managed fighters and ran a boxing school and training facility. **(Courtesy Antiquities of the Prize Ring)**

HARD-HITTING NEW YORKER. Joe Ellingsworth, a clever and scrappy middleweight from New York, was engaged as Boxing Instructor by the Southern California Athletic Club (SCAC) in Los Angeles in June of 1889. By this time in his career, he had been in the ring with Jack McAuliffe, Jack Fogarty, John Robinson, P.J. Kelly and J.K. Shell. Joe had three brothers who were also boxers - Billy, Charlie and Jack. Ellingsworth encouraged boxing in Los Angeles and surrounding cities by having some good fighters from the east come to Los Angeles. **(Courtesy Tom Scharf)**

Ellingsworth is wonderfully quick on his feet, hits very straight, and has a tremendous reach. His ducking is also remarkably clever. The first man who tackles him will find him a very awkward customer to handle.

DYNAMITE FROM THE EAST. Denny Kelliher was a popular boxer from Quincy, Massachusetts. He was a quick and devastating hitter who was capable of taking out much larger men. Jim Corbett once stated that Kelliher was one of the hardest hitters "pound for pound" that ever graced the ring

DEFEAT FOR JOE. On August 20, 1889, Denny Kelliher engaged in a desperate battle with Joe Ellingsworth at the Southern California AC. Denny finally subdued Joe after forty-three rounds of hard fighting. Here is a brief clipping from the Los Angeles Times that reports the results of the contest.

JOE ELLINGSWORTH KNOCKED OUT.

LOS ANGELES, Cal., August 21.

A fight to a finish, Marquis of Queensberry rules, for a purse of $1,500, took place at the Southern California Athletic Club last night between Joe Ellingsworth, of New York, and Denny Kelleher, of Boston. Ellingsworth was knocked out in the forty-third round by a blow on the neck.

THIRD HOME. The home of the LAAC, from 1889 to 1896, was in the Stowell Block at 226 South Spring Street. The motto "Health, Recreation, Grace and Vigor" was adopted in 1890. The men in charge felt that physical vigor was the basis for moral and bodily welfare. It was claimed that a diet of fruits and vegetables was better for the health of the athletes than raw beef. The club became the main place for physical culture in Southern California. (**Courtesy UCLA Special Collections**)

HOW SWEET IT IS. This clipping, from the Los Angeles Times, describes the rematch contest between Joe Ellingsworth and Denny Kelliher held in San Francisco on May 23, 1890, nine months after the first bout. Ellingsworth gained revenge when he knocked Kelliher out in the fiftieth round.

PRIZE FIGHTING IN SAN FRANCISCO.

Another Exhibition Before the Golden Gate Athletic Club.

SAN FRANCISCO, Cal., May 24.

Denny Kelliher, of Boston, and Joe Ellingsworth, of Los Angeles, middleweights, fought fifty rounds at the Golden Gate Athletic Club last night for a purse of $1,000. Kelliher was knocked out in the fiftieth round. Ellingsworth did most of the leading throughout the fight, which on the part of Kelliher was a waiting one. Ellingsworth drew blood from Kelliher's nose and mouth in the sixteenth round, and by jabbing so weakened the Bostonian that in the forty-third round he was knocked through the ropes, and in the forty-seventh was assisted to his seat by his second. A short right hander on the jaw in the forty-ninth round sent him to the floor, and from that time on he was at the mercy of Ellingsworth, who knocked him down three times before the fight was declared ended in his favor.

A GAME MAN. Billy Manning (on the right) traveled to Minneapolis and on March 19, 1891, tangled with the talented Charley Johnson at the Twin City Athletic Club. The battle lasted twenty rounds with Johnson stopping Billy in the last session.

BAD LUCK FOR JOE. In a game and clever fight held at the Pastime Social Club in Los Angeles on September 17, 1891, Gus Hergett outdid Joe Soto and won by a clean knock out in round seventeen. The last round saw some vicious exchanges of punches. Soto landed a solid blow to Hergett's jaw. Gus answered with stiff blows and Soto dropped like a log. In spite of the loss, Soto was impressive enough to land a fight against George "Kid" Lavigne on November 20, 1891 in San Francisco. Lavigne, future Lightweight Champion, won in thirty rounds.

HERGETT-SOTO.

Clever Seventeen-round Contest—Hergett the Victor.

The long anticipated fight between Joe Soto and Gus Hergett came off last evening before the Pastime Social Club in their rooms in the Downey Block.

A large crowd were present and the best of order was maintained. Several comical but uninteresting preliminary events between four sets of lightweights took place before the men entered the ring.

TOUGH BILLY. Billy Manning (on the left) gets set to spar with Eddie Robinson. On October 23, 1891 at the Pastime Social Club, Manning knocked out William Lewis in ten rounds. A purse of $500 was at stake. Manning was down once in the second round, twice in the eighth and once in the ninth. Lewis was down once in the eighth, twice in the ninth and three times in the tenth. **(Courtesy Antiquities of the Prize Ring)**

TITLE CLAIMANT. George LaBlanche was a tough welterweight and middleweight fighter of the 1882-1903 years. LaBlanche knocked out "Nonpareil" Jack Dempsey on August 27, 1889 to claim the Middleweight Championship of the World. However, the claim was not universally recognized because it was decided that LaBlanche used an illegal punch, the "pivot" blow. George visited Los Angeles during 1892 and, unfortunately, lost three bouts while in town.

STOCKY, POWERFUL. Frank Childs was a popular black fighter in the Los Angeles area during 1892-1893. On February 18, 1892, he knocked out George LaBlanche in three rounds. On March 24, he defeated LaBlanche once again, this time on a foul in eight rounds. Later in the year, on August 30, Childs was back in the city and knocked out Al Butler in a single round and then, on November 16, stopped John Rivers in four rounds. Some historians think Childs may have fought contests in Los Angeles as early as 1889. **(Courtesy Chicago Historical Society)**

CALM DOWN, MR. CORBETT. Heavyweight title contender, Jim Corbett, on the far left, was alarmed at the sight of a pistol being pointed at him in San Bernardino during early June of 1892. Corbett's sparring partner, Jim Daly, standing behind Corbett, took all comers in boxing contests. A black fellow named Tate accepted the challenge and, during an exchange of punches, floored Daly. Corbett jumped into the ring, knocked Tate down and kicked him. Then, a lawman entered the ring and pulled a gun on Corbett, ordering him to back away. That man was Virgil Earp, brother of the famous Marshall, Wyatt Earp.

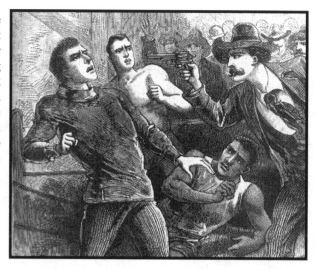

AUSTRALIAN VISITOR. Billy "Shadow" Maber did not look like a fighter but he was a long-armed, sizzling hitter who could certainly handle his fists. Maber came to America from down under in the year 1891 and found his way to Los Angeles during early 1892. While here, he knocked out Jimmy Lawson on March 3 and won over Frank Purcell on May 11. Maber went on to tangle with "Mysterious" Billy Smith in Portland, Oregon on September 20, 1892 and was subdued in twenty-six rounds. On February 28, 1893, Maber knocked out Danny Needham in thirty-five rounds in Butte, Montana and on September 21 of the same year, knocked out George LaBlanche in Minneapolis in two rounds. **(Courtesy Antiquities of the Prize Ring)**

AN ALL-TIME GREAT. Peter Jackson was one of the great heavyweights of all time. Arguably, he was the greatest fighter during the 1890s. When Jackson came to America from Australia, he toured the United States taking on all-comers in exhibitions. Many times, he boxed his opponent with his right-hand barred, meaning he could not use that hand.

PETER JACKSON.

The Colored Champion at Turnverein Hall Last Evening.

A very mixed crowd of fully eight hundred men assembled at Turnverein Hall last night to greet the acknowledged pugilistic champion of Australia, Peter Jackson, on the occasion of his initial appearance in this city.

In addition to the attraction offered by the presence of the man whom ex-Champion John J. Sullivan refused to meet on account of his color, an interesting programme was provided for the entertainment of the crowd, consisting of a number of more or less exciting set-tos, which admirably served their purpose in keeping the spectators in good humor, and one of them was as pretty an exhibition of boxing as has been seen in this city for some time past.

EXHIBITION. Jackson boxed a four round exhibition against Frank Childs on January 19, 1893 in the "City of Angels" at Turnverein Hall and was dominant. The crowd consisted of at least 800 men.

HE FOUGHT MOST OF THE GOOD, BIG MEN. Hank Griffin and Frank Childs fought to a twenty round draw in April of 1893 in Los Angeles. During his career, Griffin fought the great Jack Johnson on at least two occasions and also tangled with Jim Jeffries, Jack Munroe and "Denver" Ed Martin. Griffin fought on a number of fight cards promoted by "Uncle" Tom McCarey, his manager. **(Courtesy Antiquities of the Prize Ring)**

MAJOR INFLUENCE. Frank A. Garbutt was prominent in business and sports in Southern California during the 1890s and the first half of the Twentieth Century. He was a major player in the industries of oil, moving pictures and aviation. He also found time to be a driving force in the Los Angeles Athletic Club (LAAC) for nearly fifty years. The club had a tremendous amateur boxing program and owned the famed Olympic Auditorium. Consequently, Garbutt became an important "behind-the-scenes" figure in both amateur and professional boxing in Los Angeles.

SIR WILLIAM. Billy Gallagher (circled) was a capable welterweight fighter during the 1890's. In addition to his ring battles, he was boxing instructor at the Los Angeles Athletic Club and he handled the affairs of young Jim Jeffries. Reportedly, Gallagher took the aspiring fighter on an early career tour through New Mexico, Arizona and Southern California. **(Courtesy Antiquities of the Prize Ring)**

HARD FOUGHT DRAW. Billy Gallagher fought thirty-five rounds against Joe Cotton on November 14, 1894 to earn a "draw" decision. Gallagher dominated the contest and injured his right hand in round twenty-five but fought cleverly after this and was still the better man.

HE TAUGHT THE BEST. DeWitt Van Court was a director at both the pioneer Olympic Club of San Francisco and its southern version, the Los Angeles Athletic Club. He was hired as a boxing instructor by the latter in 1896. Van Court wrote articles on various boxing topics for the Los Angeles Times during the teens and in 1926 wrote a book on boxing in California.

LACC BOXERS. The LAAC was awe-inspiring with its hallowed halls, walls and entryways. All were neat, clean and brightly polished. Its quiet atmosphere was impressive. Some of the young men who learned their boxing skills here were impressive too. Shown are some club champions in their respective weight classes. Top row (left to right) are Walla Wheeler, featherweight; R.J. LaLande, welterweight; Sam Coulter, lightweight. Bottom row (left to right) are A.C. Jardsierff, heavyweight; DeWitt Van Court, boxing instructor; Cliff Reuman, middleweight.

ONE TOUGH MAN. James J. Jeffries, the great heavyweight champion, did his early fighting in the Los Angeles area around 1895-1896. Throughout his life, DeWitt Van Court maintained that Jeffries was the greatest heavyweight fighter he had ever seen. Said Van Court in one published work, "I was with James J. Jeffries when he first started to box. I was with him when he won the Championship, and I was with him when he lost it, and besides being the greatest heavyweight champion that ever lived, he is today and has been all his life a man among men, a true friend with a heart as big as his body." **(Courtesy Bruce Jarvis)**

JOHN BRINK AND THE JEFFRIES CROUCH. One LAAC member who boxed at the club regularly was John Brink. He sometimes sparred with the young Jeffries. On a particular afternoon, Brink landed a blow to Jeffries' midsection that doubled him over. Jim continued to box in the bent over fashion and hit effectively with powerful blows while, at the same time, protecting himself. The formidable "Jeffries Crouch" was born. See Jeffries' comments below.

I made the discovery during a bout with John Brink, who refereed the first professional fight of my life; the one with Griffin.

Brink was a fast and rather clever boxer, much older and more experienced than I and a master of the art of infighting. He knew all the tricks and was a remarkable teacher of boxing. We were engaged in a friendly match and during a mixup he hit me a hard left hand hook to the liver

HOME NUMBER FOUR. The home of the Los Angeles Athletic Club from 1896 to 1901 and from 1906 to 1911 was located on the Wilson Block at 534 1/2 South Spring Street. The Manhattan Gymnasium occupied the Club's quarters afterwards. (**Courtesy UCLA Special Collections**)

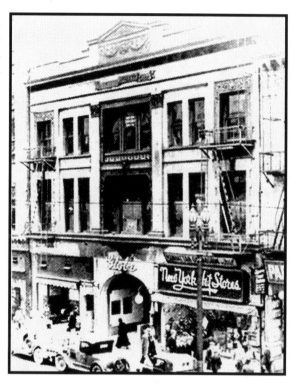

AN EVENING OF SPARRING. In the photo to the left, the January 5, 1897 program displays Billy Gallagher (to the right) and Jim Burns of Chicago (on the left). They were scheduled to "spar" for 15 rounds in the Gymnasium of the Los Angeles Athletic Club.

A YOUNG STAR RISES. Here is part of an advertisement for the bouts at Hazard's Pavilion on April 27, 1897. Jim Jeffries was scheduled to fight Billy Woods, from Denver.

Los Angeles Times, April 28, 1897

A BOXING CARNIVAL.

FOUR INOFFENSIVE BOXING MATCHES AT THE PAVILION.

A Thrilling Reproduction of the Last Scene of the Great Corbett-Fitzsimmons Fight.

JEFFRIES PUMMELS WOODS.

BOXING CARNIVAL. Here is a report from the Times, April 28, 1897. At the very bottom can be seen the words "Jeffries Pummels Woods." The two men fought six rounds in an exhibition. Jeffries dominated. During the last round, Woods played the part of Jim Corbett while Jeffries assumed the role of Bob Fitzsimmons. They performed a re-enactment of the recent March 17 Heavyweight Championship bout in Carson City, Nevada.

WORLD CHAMPION. The first World Boxing Champion from Southern California was "Solly" Smith. On October 4, 1897, Smith (right) defeated George Dixon (left) in twenty rounds in San Francisco and claimed the Featherweight Championship of the World.

TOUGH CUSTOMER. Jack Stelzner (on the right) faces the great Bob Fitzsimmons (left). Stelzner started out as a middleweight and grew into a heavyweight. He was the trainer and sparring partner of Fitzsimmons for several years. Stelzner was "willing" and liked to trade punches. His greatest asset was the way he responded to punishment and came back fighting. Jack was scheduled to fight Jim Jeffries on February 22, 1897 but the contest was cancelled due to a training injury he [Jack] experienced. **(Courtesy Antiquities of the Prize Ring)**

STELZNER TAKES McAULIFFE TO SCHOOL. Here is the headline from a Los Angeles Times article reporting the fight on October 19, 1897. Jack Stelzner defeated big Joe McAuliffe in fifteen rounds at Hazard's Pavilion. Jack was outweighed by more than 40 pounds but outboxed his man to gain the victory. Stelzner scored first blood in round two and had McAuliffe bleeding time and again during the contest. There were no knockdowns but Jack went to the floor in round seven following a hard right hand swing. Referee John Brink awarded the decision to Stelzner.

STELZNER WINS.

OUTPOINTS THE MISSION GIANT LAST NIGHT.

A Clever Boxing Bout Which Was Strictly on Its Merits Throughout.

M'AULIFFE MUCH TOO SLOW.

BOTH MEN WERE IN SPLENDID CONDITION.

A FISTIC FIZZLE.

ANOTHER HAZARD'S PAVILION BOXING CONTEST.

Goddard Gives Up the Fight Before Jeffries Has Time to Do Any Damage—Two Preliminary Knock-outs.

JEFFRIES WINS. In a disappointing contest, Jim Jeffries defeated Joe Goddard on February 28, 1898 at Hazard's Pavilion and took another step up the Heavyweight ladder towards the championship. The fight received a lot of publicity but Goddard did little effective fighting and Jeffries knocked him around. Joe quit in his corner after the third round. Referee John Brink declared Jeffries the winner and said that Goddard would get no money for the poor fight he put up. Joe then jumped up and squared off against Jeffries. The two men began fighting but Goddard was too tempestuous and Brink stopped it for good.

FUTURE CHAMPION. Just a little over 15 months later, Jeffries (below) captured the Heavyweight Championship of the World. **(Courtesy Bruce Jarvis)**

Chapter Two

The Tom McCarey Era

1901-1914

During most of the Nineteenth Century and the first two decades of the Twentieth Century, professional boxing was illegal in much of the United States. After the turn of the century, there were legal restrictions imposed in the states of New York and Illinois, which meant that major bouts could not take place in Chicago or New York City, the two largest cities in the United States. As a result, more major bouts took place in California from 1901 to late 1914 than in any other state. San Francisco was one of the major boxing centers in the world during the 1880s and 1890s and became even more important, starting in 1901.

With an exploding population, Los Angeles became a major boxing venue for the first time. The man who put the city on the map was Tom McCarey, who was around thirty years old in 1901. He staged boxing cards in the area for nearly fifteen years. During his time, many important bouts were held in Los Angeles and nearby Vernon and witnessed by large crowds.

McCarey staged the first World Championship bouts in the area and also promoted many other contests. He became one of the great boxing promoters of the period along with "Sunshine" Jim Coffroth of San Francisco, Tex Rickard and Hugh McIntosh of Australia.

McCarey and other businessmen established the Century Athletic Club with McCarey acting as the manager. In the first show of the club, "Solly" Smith fought Joe Bernstein in the main event staged at Hazard's Pavilion in Los Angeles on May of 1901.

The Century Athletic Club enjoyed a great deal of success at Hazard's Pavilion. Many of the boxing shows featured some fine black boxers - Jack Johnson, Sam McVea, "Denver" Ed Martin, Billy Woods, Joe Walcott, the Dixie Kid (Aaron Brown) and Frank Childs. Other noted boxers who fought at Hazard's Pavilion during the period included Charles "Kid" McCoy, Jack "Twin" Sullivan, Johnny Reagan, Frankie Neil, Al Neill, Kid Carter and Billy DeCoursey.

There was a short period of time, in late 1903, when boxing cards were not staged in Los Angeles due to an ordinance passed by the City Council that prohibited professional boxing. The ordinance was ruled unconstitutional in 1904 and boxing cards resumed at Hazard's Pavilion late that year and continued until the Temple Baptist Church leased the pavilion years later.

In 1905, McCarey staged boxing cards under the auspices of the Pacific Athletic Club at a new arena with a reported capacity of 6,500 in the Naud Junction area of Los Angeles. Despite experiencing some setbacks, McCarey regularly put on bouts there until early 1911.

It appears that McCarey staged the first world title bouts in Los Angeles. In 1906, Tommy Burns won the World Heavyweight title from Marvin Hart and defended his title successfully three times during the next couple of years.

Abe Attell defended his World Featherweight title successfully seven times at McCarey's arena during 1906 and 1907. Joe Gans retained his World Lightweight title by winning a decision over George Memsic at McCarey's arena on September 27, 1907. According to some sources, there were two World Welterweight title bouts held at McCarey's arena in 1907. Mike "Twin" Sullivan won the title from Billy "Honey" Mellody and retained it by knocking out "Kid" Farmer. However, these contests are not universally recognized as World Championship contests.

During late 1907, there was a Los Angeles city edict mandating no-decision bouts with the maximum number of rounds set at ten. As a result, World Championship bouts were essentially eliminated within the city limits until 1925. This act presented an opportunity for the small, incorporated, industrial town of Vernon, located a few miles south of Downtown Los Angeles, to play a major role in area boxing.

Starting in 1908, Vernon became a sports center for the area for nearly two decades. From then until 1927, there were boxing cards staged in Vernon with few interruptions. Vernon also had a baseball team, the Vernon Tigers, in the Pacific Coast League from 1908 through 1925 with the exception of 1913 when the Tigers played in Venice. In addition, for a number of years, Vernon was a place where people could get an alcoholic drink.

Vernon allowed twenty-five round bouts with decisions beginning in 1908. The new Jeffries Athletic Club staged cards in an open-air arena that year, the first main event being a twenty-five rounder between Mike "Twin" Sullivan and Jimmy Gardner, held before a small crowd. However, the vast majority of the boxing cards at the new club were not successful, with the exception being the second World Middleweight bout between Billy Papke and Stanley Ketchel. The Jeffries AC went out of business in January 1909.

In 1910, Tom McCarey staged boxing cards at his arena in the Naud Junction area and at the open-air arena in Vernon. Afterwards, McCarey promoted boxing cards in Vernon on an exclusive basis. He experienced continued success and resumed staging World Championship bouts there.

McCarey's biggest drawing card proved to be "Mexican" Joe Rivers, a lightweight contender from Los Angeles. When Rivers reached his peak during the early teens, he drew very large crowds in Vernon.

Rivers' most memorable bout was against Ad Wolgast for the World Lightweight title in front of approximately 10,000 fans in Vernon on July 4, 1912. The gate for the bout was over $40,000, a record for the Los Angeles area before the **Ten-Round Era**, which began in 1925. The bout ended in the thirteenth round when both fighters were apparently knocked down at the same time. In a controversial action, Referee Jack Welsh helped Wolgast up while counting Rivers out.

During the November election of 1914, California voters passed an amendment that bouts in California would be scheduled for a maximum of only four rounds and that a boxer could not receive a prize worth more than $25. It set the stage for the **Four-Round Era** in California, which lasted until the beginning of 1925. Despite the fact that McCarey was only about 43 years old and lived another twenty years, his career as a boxing promoter ended. The new amendment also ended, for the most part, the career of another major boxing promoter, Jim Coffroth, of San Francisco. However, he did promote at least one benefit card in San Francisco during World War I.

GOING BIG TIME. Boxing in Los Angeles took on a new look as three excellent bouts were scheduled for early May of 1901. The first contest was scheduled for Turner Hall on May 3 between Bill Walsh and Kid Long with a 128 pound limit. On May 7, at Hazard's Pavilion, two heavyweights, Hank Griffin and Joe Kennedy, were set to tangle. And, on May 10, also at Hazard's, former Featherweight Champion, "Solly" Smith, was to meet New Yorker, Joe Bernstein. Reportedly, World Champion Terry McGovern would fight the winner for the Featherweight Championship. All three bouts were set for twenty rounds.

FISTICAL CARNIVAL.

Three Days of Fighting, Fiesta Week.

Terry McGovern is to Be on Hand.

Griffin and Kennedy, Smith and Bernstein, Walsh and Long Matched.

FIRST SHOW. The first boxing card of the Century Athletic Club was staged at Hazard's Pavilion on May 10, 1901. The main event was between Joe Bernstein (left) and "Solly" Smith. It ended in a draw after twenty rounds of boxing. In a repeat, the two men fought another twenty round draw on June 18. Smith was the harder puncher but Bernstein was better at infighting and defense. The June 18 card was important historically because it was the start of Tom McCarey's reign as a boxing promoter in the Los Angeles area. McCarey was about thirty years old at this point in time and his career as a boxing promoter continued until late 1914. **(Courtesy Antiquities of the Prize Ring)**

FOUGHT FOR THE BLACK HEAVYWEIGHT CROWN. "Denver" Ed Martin was a good boxer who had fast hands and moved well. His weakness was his inability to take solid punches. He first appeared in Los Angeles on October 2, 1901, when he knocked out Hank Griffin in seven rounds. He was back for an extended stay two years later. During 1903, on February 5, he lost a twenty round decision to Jack Johnson for the "Colored" Heavyweight Championship of the World and on September 15, was knocked out by Sam McVea in one round. During 1904, on August 12, he avenged his loss to McVea by taking a ten round

decision but, on October 18, was knocked out by Jack Johnson in two rounds at Hazard's Pavilion with the famous referee, Charles Eyton, officiating. **(Courtesy Chicago Historical Society)**

TRICKY GUY. Frank Fields was a scrappy middleweight who fought often in the Oxnard, Los Angeles and San Bernardino areas from 1901 to 1904. A boxer with a good punch, Fields stopped "Utah" Bob Thompson in six rounds in Oxnard in 1902, owned wins over Jack "Kid" Lavelle and Buck Stelzer in 1903 and earned a victory over "Kid" Sullivan in 1904. **(Courtesy Antiquities of the Prize Ring)**

DYNAMITE IN A SMALL PACKAGE. The great Joe Walcott, a fighter that many boxing historians rate as the greatest welterweight of all time, appeared only once in Los Angeles. On April 2, 1903, Walcott, who was the World Welterweight Champion at the time, and Billy Woods fought to a twenty round draw in a bout at Hazard's Pavilion. Some sources recognize this contest as a World Welterweight title contest. **(Courtesy Antiquities of the Prize Ring)**

JOHNSON STILL "IT."

Gets Decision Over McVey After Punching the Oxnard Man Through Twenty Terrible Rounds—Never a Scratch for Champion.

BIG, BLACK AND POWERFUL. Sam McVea (sometimes spelled McVey) came roaring out of Oxnard in 1902 with a series of knockout wins. Unbeaten, he tangled with Jack Johnson for the "Colored" Heavyweight Championship on February 26, 1903 and experienced his first loss. After this, Sam scored two more knockouts and then tried Johnson once more - on October 27, 1903 at Hazard's Pavilion; again, for the "Colored" Heavyweight title, again, another loss. In the sketch to the left, McVea is on the left receiving a right hand punch from Johnson. Charles Eyton (far right) was the third man in the ring for this contest. McVea gave it one more try against Johnson on April 22, 1904, but lost. He learned his lesson well and never again fought Jack. But, he went on to become a great fighter and along with Johnson, Sam Langford and Joe Jeannette formed an outstanding foursome of super black fighters during the early years of the century.

McCAREY AND SOME OF HIS FIGHTERS. Pictured here is Tom McCarey and his small son (circled) along with a number of fighters that McCarey handled. "Uncle Tom" was the top man in Los Angeles boxing during this time period. His son, Leo, went on to become one of the greatest directors of the Classic Hollywood era. His films were very successful and he was admired by his colleagues. Leo won three Oscars and was nominated 36 times for his films. **(Courtesy Antiquities of the Prize Ring)**

A SCRAPPY ONE. Billy Woods, a talented welterweight and middleweight, was a popular fighter in the Los Angeles area. Woods was quick and could box as well as punch. During his career, Woods fought such men as Joe Walcott, "Rough House" Burns, Mike Schreck, Joe Millet, Nick Burley and Dave Barry. On September 16, 1904 in Seattle, Woods boxed a fifteen round draw against future heavyweight champion, Tommy Burns. "Uncle" Tom McCarey managed Woods during his early career. Later, George William "Biddy" Bishop handled his affairs. **(Courtesy Kevin Smith)**

SUPPORT FOR JOHNSON. Jim Jeffries, like the heavyweight champions before him, drew the "color line" when it came to fighting black opponents for the heavyweight crown. Nevertheless, the Los Angeles Times newspaper, as well as many California fans, clamored for a fight between Jeffries and Jack Johnson, the "Colored Heavyweight Champion."

P UBLIC REFUSES TO
   ACCEPT COLOR LINE.

'DE CHAMP" WILL HAVE TO GET
OFF HIS HIGH HORSE.

Sporting World Will Insist Upon One
Meeting Between Jeffries and Black
Heavyweight Champion for the World's
Title—Other Pugilistic Happenings.

Jeff says he will retire before he will meet a colored man for the title. If he does that, he will have to retire from the stage as well, and he figures on doing no such foolish thing.

Jeffries has been talking to eastern reporters about going to Africa to shoot lions and clean up some heavyweights there. First he better bag one or two African heavyweights on this side. He can whip any man in the business if he will.

THE KID WITH FAST HANDS. Aaron Lister Brown (on the left), shown here with Sam Langford, fought as the "Dixie Kid." He was born in Missouri but fought mostly in Los Angeles and California during his early career. Thirty-two of his first thirty-three bouts took place in the Golden State. On April 29, 1904, he defeated Joe Walcott in twenty rounds in San Francisco for the Welterweight Championship of the World. Brown was quick and agile and well-known for fighting with his hands held low, often dangling at his sides. During his career, he defeated such men as Al Neil, Mose LaFontise, Joe Grim, George Cole, Jeff Clark, Georges Carpentier, Johnny Summers, George Gunther, Young Loughrey, Jack Meekins, Arthur Evernden, Dick Nelson, Jack Goldswain and Fred Drummond. **(Courtesy Antiquities of the Prize Ring)**

GREAT PROMOTER. "Uncle" Tom McCarey built the Pacific Athletic Club Pavilion in the Naud Junction area of Downtown Los Angeles around 1905. He staged many championship bouts and twenty rounders until contests were limited to ten rounds by a city ordinance. The Jeffries Athletic Club was built later in Vernon, a suburb of Los Angeles. It was an open air arena and bouts could have a limit of 45 rounds as prescribed by state law.

DAPPER DRESSER. Frankie Neil, the man with the amazing left hand, won the Bantamweight title in 1903 and defended it twice at Hazard's Pavilion that year. The following year, he lost the crown to Joe Bowker in London, England. Neil was scheduled to fight Abe Attell in a World Featherweight title bout on April 20, 1906 at Naud Junction but the San Francisco Earthquake occurred on April 18 and the bout was postponed indefinitely. Neil left town shortly afterwards. Tom McCarey then scheduled Attell against "Kid" Herman in a Featherweight title bout on May 11 at Naud Junction. The result was a draw in twenty rounds and Attell retained his title. McCarey finally got Neil and Attell together on July 4 at Naud. Attell won a twenty round decision. McCarey later called this the greatest featherweight bout he ever saw. What a donnybrook this would have been when both were in their prime as champions. **(Courtesy Antiquities of the Prize Ring)**

LITTLE MAN, BIG PUNCH. Tommy Burns (left), he of the terrible right hand punch, is shown posing with "Philadelphia" Jack O'Brien. Burns fought for the Heavyweight Championship of the World four times in Los Angeles during 1906-1907. In these battles, Burns won the heavyweight crown when he beat Marvin Hart, defended the title when he knocked out "Fireman" Jim Flynn, fought a twenty round draw against O'Brien in which he retained the championship belt and then defeated O'Brien in another title defense. **(Courtesy Antiquities of the Prize Ring)**

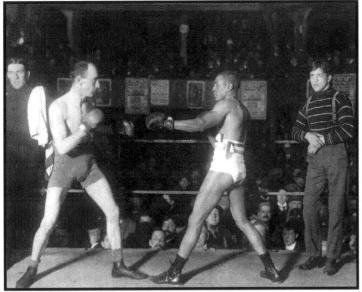

THE MASTER. The great Joe Gans (on the right) stopped Mike "Twin" Sullivan (left) in ten rounds on March 17, 1906 at Chutes Park in a non-McCarey promotion. Many historians call it a Welterweight Championship contest. Then, on September 27, 1907, in a Lightweight Championship bout held at the Naud Junction Pavilion, Gans defeated George Memsic in twenty rounds to retain that title. **(Courtesy Tom Scharf)**

LITTLE WARRIOR. Charlie "Kid" Dalton was a good inside fighter who waged many battles in the Los Angeles area during the first twenty years of the century. His major wins came against Danny Webster, Jack Clifford and Rudi Unholz (twice). He also fought draws with Webster and Stanley "Kid" Yoakum.

ONE OF THE GREATEST. After his July 4, 1906 title bout with Frankie Neil, Abe Attell (left) fought five Featherweight title fights at the Naud Junction Pavilion during 1906-1907. On October 30, 1906, he defended his title and won a twenty round verdict against Harry Baker (right) and on December 7, retained his crown against Jimmy Walsh by an eighth round knockout. In a rematch with Baker, in January of 1907, Abe knocked out his man in eight rounds to remain Champion. Shortly afterwards, on May 24, he won a twenty round decision against Benny "Kid" Solomon and on October 29, he knocked out Freddie Weeks in four rounds. **(Courtesy Antiquities of the Prize Ring)**

ONE OF THE TWINS. Mike "Twin" Sullivan appeared in the Los Angeles area three times after his March 17, 1906 loss to Joe Gans. On April 23, 1907, Sullivan defeated Billy "Honey" Mellody in twenty rounds to win the Welterweight Championship of the World as recognized by the state of California. Seven months later, on November 27, he stopped Kid Farmer in thirteen rounds (see the article to the right). Then, he defeated Jimmy Gardner in twenty-five rounds in Vernon on April 22, 1908 in a Welterweight title defense.

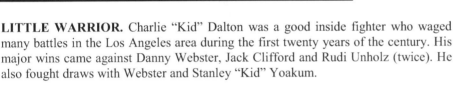

FARMER EASY FOR SULLIVAN.

Plays With the Kid Through Twelve Slow Rounds.

Mike "Twin" Sullivan played with Kid Farmer for twelve rounds last night at the Pacific Athletic Club, and then when he had him all but out in the thirteenth round, Referee Charley Eyton stopped the uneven contest and gave the decision to Sullivan, thus saving Farmer a knockout.

GO WEST, YOUNG MAN. George Memsic (Jimmy Burns) was born in Streator, Illinois and invaded Los Angeles in the fall of 1906, where he scored a victory over Charlie Neary. He continued his streak of wins in the area in 1907 with successes against "Cyclone" Johnny Thompson and the Montana Kid. On September 27, he met with a loss at the Naud Junction Pavilion when he tangled with Joe Gans in a twenty rounder for the Lightweight crown. Over the next three years, he fought battles here against Rudi Unholz, Phil Brock, Clarence English, Freddie Welsh, Ad Wolgast, Frank Picato and Lew Powell.

HERE THEY GO AGAIN. Jack "Twin" Sullivan (left) and Hugo Kelly (right) were contenders for the middleweight title that Tommy Ryan vacated in 1907. They engaged in several contests against each other and each man won once. The other contests were draws. Two of these were held in Los Angeles during 1906-1907 and each ended in a twenty round draw. Here, they are seen squaring off in one of the bouts in the *City of Angels*.

BIG JIM'S CAFÉ. Above is a view of the interior of Jim Jeffries' Cafe in Los Angeles during 1907. The "Gentleman's Cafe" of Jeffries & Kipper was located at 326 South Spring Street in Los Angeles. The "Big Fellow" dropped in regularly.

MORE POCKET MONEY. Jim Jeffries made money refereeing boxing contests after his retirement in 1905. He officiated a number of world championship contests and even handled amateur bouts. Seen below, decked out in his derby hat, Jeffries handled some bouts in the Boxing Carnival at Chutes Park during Fleet Week, April 18-25, 1908.

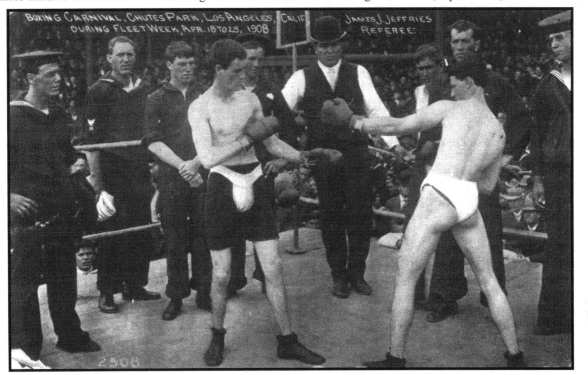

JEFFRIES ATHLETIC CLUB. Vernon allowed 25-round bouts with decisions, beginning in 1908, and the first bout at the new open-air Jeffries AC arena (left) was held on April 22, 1908. The main event was a twenty-five round contest between Mike "Twin" Sullivan and Jimmy Gardner in front of a small crowd. Unfortunately, the vast majority of the new club's boxing cards were not successful, with the big exception of the second World Middleweight bout between Billy Papke and Stanley Ketchel. The Jeffries AC went out of business in January of 1909.

POOR FIGHT. Some 600-800 boxing fans shivered through three hours of cold to watch the rather dull initial fight card at the Jeffries AC. Two boring fights led off the evening, followed by the Sullivan-Gardner encounter that was promoted as the Welterweight Championship of the World. Sullivan completely dominated Gardner over twenty-five rounds to capture the decision (see the article to the right).

GARDNER LOST TO SULLIVAN.

Poor Fight for First Card of Jeffries's New Club.

Small Crowd of Sports Have Three Cold Hours.

At the end, Jeffries gave the decision to Sullivan, and from the appearance of the fighters any one but a blind man would have called the twin the winner

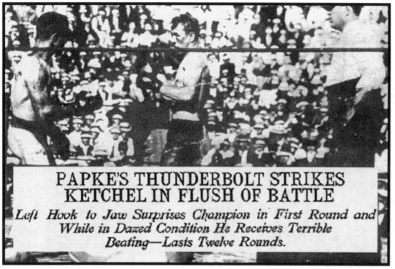

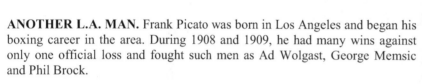

PAPKE'S THUNDERBOLT STRIKES
KETCHEL IN FLUSH OF BATTLE
*Left Hook to Jaw Surprises Champion in First Round and
While in Dazed Condition He Receives Terrible
Beating—Lasts Twelve Rounds.*

A BIG UPSET. Billy Papke (on the left) shocked the world on September 7, 1908, when he stopped Stanley Ketchel in twelve rounds to capture the Middleweight Championship staged by the Jeffries Athletic Club in Vernon. Jim Jeffries (far right) was the referee. Ketchel regained his title on November 26, a little more than two months later, by knocking out Papke in eleven rounds in Colma.

ANOTHER L.A. MAN. Frank Picato was born in Los Angeles and began his boxing career in the area. During 1908 and 1909, he had many wins against only one official loss and fought such men as Ad Wolgast, George Memsic and Phil Brock.

Memsic was made a 10 to 9 favorite yesterday over Frank Picato for their fight Friday night by the recording of several bets, but the general run of fans figure that the chances of each of the fighters is equal, as Memsic can make 133 readily and already in his training he has been down to the 135 mark and will simply need to do regular exercise to be in prime shape, though the added two pounds will do him little good.

On the other hand, Picato will be greatly benefited by the increase in weight over the lightweight limit and he will be seen at his best at 135 pounds. Picato has decided to take on Rawhide Kelly to look after his interests in the training camp and the experience of this old war horse will add to Frank's chances of success when he meets Memsic in the ring Friday evening.

MORE ABOUT FRANK. In 1910, Picato fought his last bouts in Los Angeles - a "no decision" contest against George Memsic on January 28 (see the prefight article to the left) and a six round knockout of Kid Burns on July 9. Frank boxed in Australia in 1911 and most of 1912. He returned to America in August of 1912 for a few contests and was back in Australia in 1913 where he finished out his career.

BEAT THE BATTLER. Shown here, Ad Wolgast (foreground) is playing handball with Patsy Kline at Jack Doyle's training camp in 1911. On February 22, 1910, Wolgast defeated Battling Nelson to capture the Lightweight Championship. A real warrior, Wolgast defended his crown four times during 1911, once at the Vernon Arena when he stopped George Memsic in nine rounds. He had appeared often in Los Angeles during 1908-1909 but his most famous fight was yet to come. **(Courtesy Antiquities of the Prize Ring)**

A YOUNG CHAMPION. On the same day, February 22, 1910, that Wolgast defeated Nelson, Frankie Conley (above left) knocked out Monte Attell (right) in forty-two rounds in Vernon to claim the Bantamweight Championship. Conley was a nineteen year old at the time but completely dominated Attell throughout the contest. The next year, 1911, was a bad one for Conley. He won only one fight in seven tries. He did manage two draws. Then, on January 1, 1912, in Vernon, he was knocked out by "Mexican" Joe Rivers in eleven rounds.

YO GONNA GIT IT TODAY. Sam Langford (next to the announcer) looked on as "Fireman" Jim Flynn was introduced for their bout on March 17, 1910 in Vernon. Just five weeks earlier, many newspapers had declared that Flynn bested Langford in a ten rounder. This time, Sam finished Flynn in eight rounds to remove all doubt as to the winner. (**Courtesy Antiquities of the Prize Ring**)

MOUNTAIN MAN. Always a lover of the outdoors - hunting, fishing, hiking and camping, Jim Jeffries spent as much time as he could in the wilderness and enjoyed every minute of it. In the mean time, the boxing world was gaining on him. Jim became ring rusty while others made strides in developing their skills to match his.

TAKE A NAP. Sam Langford turns to his left as Jim Barry hits the canvas in their April 14, 1910 match in Vernon. Langford knocked Barry out in round sixteen. A legendary fighter, Sam appeared in Los Angeles, Vernon, San Diego, Venice, Huntington Beach and San Fernando on many occasions during his career and lost only once – in 1924, when Sam was near the end of his ring days after 22 years of fighting. **(Courtesy Antiquities of the Prize Ring)**

SURPRISE, IT'S ME. Willie Ritchie (left) tangled with Freddie Welsh (right) on November 30, 1911 at the Vernon Arena and lost a competitive twenty round decision. Ritchie had ridden a train all night to see Welsh fight against Ad Wolgast. When he arrived, he learned that Wolgast was ill and could not fight. Willie took his place. Two years and seven months later, Welsh again defeated Ritchie in twenty rounds to capture the Lightweight Championship of the World.

CHAMPIONSHIP REPEAT. A number of celebrities gathered before the Johnny Coulon-Frankie Conley Bantamweight Championship fight on February 3, 1912 in Vernon. In the above photo, left to right, are Freddie Welsh, Conley, Jack "One-Round" Hogan, Ad Wolgast, Coulon, Abe Attell, "Harlem" Tommy Murphy, Johnny Kilbane, Tommy Kilbane and "Mexican" Joe Rivers. In the contest, the outstanding and seasoned Coulon outboxed Conley to gain a twenty round decision and the title. It was the second meeting between the two men who had fought for the same title a year earlier in New Orleans. Coulon also won that one in twenty rounds. **(Courtesy Antiquities of the Prize Ring)**

KILBANE WINS THE TITLE. On February 22, 1912 at the Vernon Arena, Johnny Kilbane (left) defeated Abe Attell in twenty rounds to capture the Featherweight Championship of the World. Fourteen months later, on April 29, 1913 at the Arena, Kilbane and Johnny Dundee fought to a twenty round draw with the Featherweight Championship at stake. Kilbane retained his title.

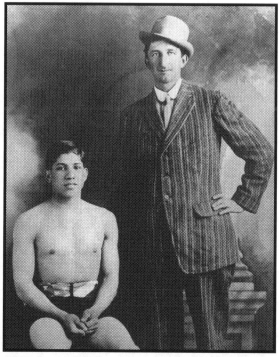

MEXICAN JOE AND HIS MANAGER? "Mexican" Joe Rivers (Jose Ybarra) was a very popular Los Angeles lightweight. During 1910-1912, he appeared in Vernon frequently and fought such men as Danny Webster, Johnny Kilbane, Tommy Dixon, Joe "Kid" Coster, Joe Mandot, Ad Wolgast and Frankie Conley. During his career, which lasted into 1924, Rivers went on to battle such big name fighters as Leach Cross, Knockout Brown, Willie Ritchie, Freddie Welsh, Willie Beecher, Johnny Dundee, Frankie Callahan, "Oakland" Frankie Burns, Stanley "Kid" Yoakum, Bobby Waugh, Joe Benjamin, Phil Salvadore, Richie Mitchell and Bobby Harper. He engaged in two world title bouts but was unsuccessful. Shown here, "Mexican" Joe is seated, in his boxing attire. His friend in the spiffy duds is unknown. Perhaps, he is Joe Levy, Joe's manager. **(Courtesy Clay Moyle)**

AT DOYLE'S. A big fight crowd always gathered at Jack Doyle's saloon in Vernon on fight day. **(Courtesy Antiquities of the Prize Ring)**

SHOW TIME. On July 4, 1912, the "Mexican" Joe Rivers-Ad Wolgast fight was held at the Vernon Arena. Thousands of fans showed up for the contest. Both men were familiar to local fans. This contest turned out to be an exciting encounter.

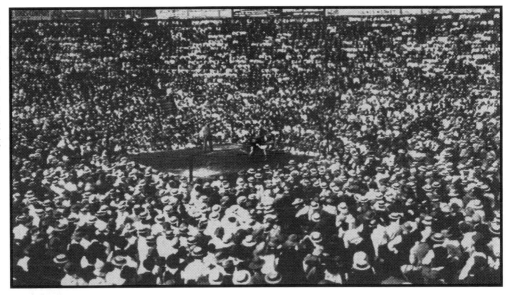

ROWDY AFFAIR. In a rough and tumble contest, Wolgast (on top) defeated Rivers in thirteen rounds for the Lightweight Championship of the World. In a controversial decision, referee Jack Welsh (standing) declared Wolgast the winner by knockout. Each man had landed a crucial blow simultaneously and both went down. Welsh assisted Wolgast up as he counted.

CHEATING GOING ON. Here is a cartoon that described the Wolgast-Rivers bout and depicted referee Welsh escaping an upset crowd.

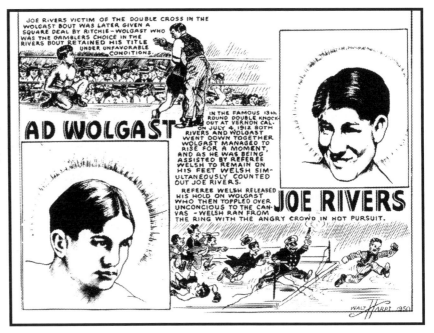

MANDOT-RIVERS #2. In Vernon, on Thanksgiving Day, 1912, "Mexican" Joe Rivers (left) tangled with Joe Mandot, a fighter from New Orleans who boasted 56 bouts to his credit with only a handful of losses. Rivers won a twenty round decision to avenge an earlier loss to Mandot that took place on September 2, 1912 in Vernon. The two men met once more, in October of 1914 in New Orleans, with Mandot gaining the win. In all, the fighters battled three times for sixty rounds. **(Courtesy Antiquities of the Prize Ring)**

HEAVY BLOW. Luther McCarty (left) was probably the best of the "White Hopes" who were after Jack Johnson's heavyweight title during the teens. He knocked out "Fireman" Jim Flynn in sixteen rounds in Vernon on December 10, 1912. On January 1, 1913 in Vernon, McCarty battled Al Palzer (shown above). The fight was stopped in round eighteen and Luther captured the White Heavyweight Championship of the World. Shortly afterwards, on May 24, 1913, McCarty died from an apparent light blow in the first round of his bout with Arthur Pelkey in Calgary, Alberta, Canada.

CAMPI BEATS BURNS. Eddie Campi (on the right) battled the talented "Jersey" Frankie Burns on March 29, 1913 in Vernon. Campi won a twenty round decision. Three months after this bout, on June 24, Campi defeated Charles Ledoux in twenty rounds in Vernon to capture the Bantamweight Championship of the World as recognized by Europe. Campi and Burns fought a non-title, fifteen-round draw just a little over six months after their first fight.

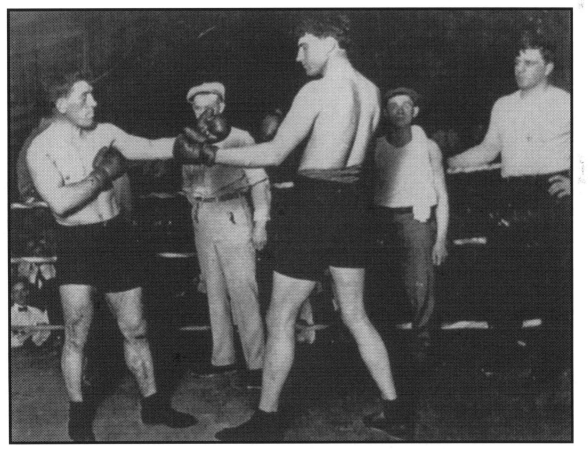

BIG AND STRONG. Jess Willard (right), the man who eventually captured the heavyweight title from Jack Johnson, faces John "Bull" Young (left). Willard knocked out Young in eleven rounds in Vernon on August 22, 1913. Young suffered a serious injury, either from the blow or striking his head on the floor. He died the next day during surgery to relieve pressure from a hemorrhage. Noah Young, his brother, was in his corner during the bout. Noah went on to become a champion weightlifter and a movie strongman in some of Harold Lloyd's movies. **(Courtesy Antiquities of the Prize Ring)**

HARD HITTING LITTLE CHAMP. On January 31, 1914, Kid Williams (back to camera) knocked out Eddie Campi (left) in twelve rounds in Vernon to win the Bantamweight Championship of the World as recognized by Europe. On June 9, 1914, also in Vernon, he knocked out Johnny Coulon in three rounds to gain full recognition as World Bantamweight Champion.

Chapter Three

The Four-Round Era

1914-1925

The 1914 anti-professional boxing amendment ushered in the **Four-Round Era** in California. Like the three-round amateur bouts of today, the four-round bouts generally featured a lot more action than the longer bouts. Boxing cards with exclusively four-round bouts were nothing new in California. Such cards had been staged in San Francisco with much success and were popular with the fans for a number of years.

Four-round boxing cards proved to be popular everywhere in California during this period. There were clubs staging boxing cards on a regular weekly basis. Due to the fact that each four-round card generally featured five to ten bouts, there were many "four-round" boxers who had hundreds of bouts.

Despite the fact that the anti-professional boxing amendment stated that a boxer could not get a prize worth more than $25 for a bout, it was no secret that many boxers received purses (often referred to as "medals") of hundreds or even thousands of dollars. Accordingly, there were many recognized professional boxers who were active in California during these years.

There were a number of small clubs that did not last very long at the beginning of the period. Newspaper coverage of these clubs was sparse and often restricted to pre-fight details with few results listed. Of these clubs, in the early four-round days, the Western Athletic Club in L.A. comes to mind. Some four-round clubs were also established in Los Angeles suburbs - in Venice and San Pedro.

A four-round club operated by Jack Doyle in Vernon emerged as the top club in the area during the teens. At that time, Doyle also operated a large drinking establishment with a huge bar. In addition, Doyle operated a training camp for boxers in Arcadia and in Vernon. There is evidence that Doyle staged boxing cards on a very small scale starting in 1912.

At the time that Hayden "Wad" Wadhams became his matchmaker in 1916, Doyle staged his boxing cards every Tuesday except on holidays. His cards were highly successful into the middle 1920s. He opened a new arena that had a capacity of 7,000 in late 1923, about ninety feet from the old structure. In 1925, the capacity of the new arena was increased to 8,500. Doyle continued to stage cards in Vernon until early 1927. Afterwards, he and his matchmaker, Wadhams, staged cards at the Olympic Auditorium.

The most popular boxer during the **Four-Round Era** in the Los Angeles area was Bert Colima, a Mexican-American boxer from Whittier. A thrilling fighter, Colima was a tremendous drawing card throughout a career that lasted from the late 1910s to the early 1930s, but most notably in Vernon during the 1920s. Other popular fighters in the area were Joe Benjamin, Phil Salvadore, Young George, Teddy Silva, Dick Hoppe and Young Nationalista.

There were a number of new boxing clubs in the Los Angeles area during the early 1920s. The most popular was the Hollywood Legion Stadium, where weekly boxing cards were held on Fridays. A semi-charitable organization, this highly successful club operated until 1959. The open-air arena was turned into a barn-like structure with a capacity of about 4,500 within a short time. A larger and much more attractive arena was built on the same spot in 1938.

At relatively big venues such as the Vernon Arena and Hollywood Legion Stadium, the usual "four-round" card had seven bouts or a total of twenty-eight scheduled rounds. Like other boxing shows, the main event was the most important bout.

A small boxing operation called the Chief Petty Officers Club staged weekly bouts in San Pedro starting in 1921 and operated until 1925. Many boxers on the San Pedro cards were serving in the United States Navy, a major source of fistic talent for the clubs on the West Coast.

As early as 1921, the Madison Square Garden Club staged cards in the Central Avenue area, where the black community in Los Angeles was located. Many of the boxers on this club's cards were black as well as white. It appears that there was little coverage on boxing cards at this venue in the local newspapers of the day. The club lasted until 1923, when a noted boxing man, Fred Winsor, attempted to stage a bout between Sam Langford and Rocco Stragmalia. Langford, a black fighter and an all-time great, was in the twilight of his career, while Stragmalia was known as a sparring partner of the World Heavyweight Champion, Jack Dempsey. Just before the bout was to begin, before a packed house, law officers stepped in to prevent the "mixed" bout. It appears that the club staged no cards after that.

Beginning in 1923, there were boxing cards staged on a weekly basis in Pasadena until the early 1930s. The most notable promoter at the latter venue was a young man named Morrie Cohen, who was known for providing a showcase for a number of black fighters before they were able to get bouts on a regular basis at the bigger venues in the area.

In late 1924, the Assembly Club staged cards in the Central Avenue area. Like the Madison Square Garden Club, the Assembly Club had many black boxers and some whites on its cards. The club ceased staging cards in 1925.

Black boxers did not fight often at the other clubs in the Los Angeles area during the **Four-Round Era**. However, during the latter part of the 1920s, black fighters appeared frequently at most venues except the Hollywood Legion Stadium, where they were not allowed to fight until 1940.

During 1924, the Wilmington Bowl was built in a suburb of Los Angeles located near Long Beach. Another arena was constructed in Culver City. Each had a capacity of about 4,000. The arena in Culver City was an impressive building but it struggled to stage cards on a regular basis until well into the 1930s. The more successful of the two was the Wilmington Bowl, which had two versions. With "Doc" Moffett as matchmaker, the first version of the Bowl operated continuously until late 1929 when the building burned to the ground.

The most infamous bout of the 1914-1925 years was between a promising young Mexican-American fighter named Tony Fuente and a tall, former heavyweight contender named Fred Fulton. This contest was held in the new arena in Culver City during November of 1924. Fuente scored a dubious knockout in the first round that was considered a fake by veteran boxing people at ringside and the fans who packed the arena. At the time of the bout, Fred Winsor managed both the arena and Fuente.

On the California election ballot in November, 1924, there was an amendment permitting professional boxing in the state, under the rule of a state athletic commission. It passed. The amendment permitted bouts with a maximum of ten scheduled rounds if there was a decision or bouts with a maximum of twelve rounds if there was no decision. As a result, cards with only four-round bouts became almost extinct in the state after 1924. However, a large number of the "four-round" boxers continued their careers.

THE MAN. Jack Doyle was a promoter of boxing and responsible for numerous innovations and improvements in the sport. His record was impressive. Among Doyle's achievements were better accommodations for boxers in their corners, orchestra seats for patrons, invitations to women to attend bouts and a security force in attendance to assure safety for the patrons. Doyle provided much financial support in the effort to pass legalization of bouts of more than four rounds. The arena he built near the close of the four round days was a wonderful structure.

JACK DOYLE'S TRAINING CAMP. Here are some views of facilities at Jack Doyle's training camp in Vernon. Images (starting in the upper left and moving clockwise) of the rubbing room, bath room, reception room and dining room are shown. Doyle is shown in the center. **(Courtesy Antiquities of the Prize Ring)**

RELAXING AT DOYLE'S. Seen here are a few fellows gathered to discuss the day's activities at Doyle's training camp. Many outstanding fighters and trainers got into shape and worked out fight strategies here.

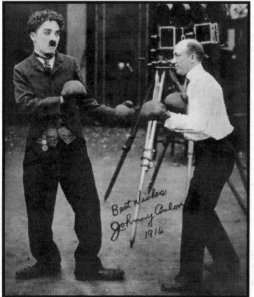

CHAPLIN CHALLENGES COULON TO A BOUT. The year is 1916 and Charlie Chaplin (left) is ready to take on former Bantamweight Champion, Johnny Coulon (right), on the set of a movie. Coulon had been displaced as Bantam king by Kid Williams in 1914 but was still plenty able. As always, Chaplin felt up to the task.

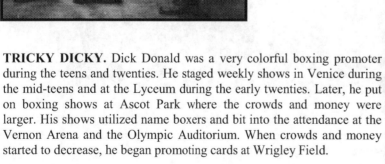

TRICKY DICKY. Dick Donald was a very colorful boxing promoter during the teens and twenties. He staged weekly shows in Venice during the mid-teens and at the Lyceum during the early twenties. Later, he put on boxing shows at Ascot Park where the crowds and money were larger. His shows utilized name boxers and bit into the attendance at the Vernon Arena and the Olympic Auditorium. When crowds and money started to decrease, he began promoting cards at Wrigley Field.

FRANKIE AND HIS WIFE. Frankie Dolan is shown here with his wife. Dolan engaged in more than 125 bouts and lost only 23 in a career that lasted from 1909-1926. In 1916, following the death of an opponent in the ring, Dolan went into retirement for nearly two years. Then, in 1918, he resumed his career and went on to win the Flyweight Championship of the Pacific Coast. Actor Charlie Chaplin was an avid fan of his. Frankie was a referee at the Olympic Auditorium and Hollywood Legion Stadium after his fighting days and also performed in motion pictures. He reportedly was the traveling secretary of actor Tom Mix and sparred frequently with the film icon. Dolan died in 1945. **(Courtesy Antiquities of the Prize Ring)**

HE SAW IT ALL. Harry Lee was a popular referee of the four-round days and the main event referee for Jack Doyle for many years. Lee presided over many bouts in which the top-notch fighters engaged. During his career as the third man, he reportedly officiated some 5,000 bouts. Harry began his athletic career as a professional baseball player and then performed as a bicyclist. Later, he acted as a trainer and worked with many outstanding boxers such as Bobby Dobbs, Joe Gans, George Dixon, Terry McGovern, Matty Mathews, Leach Cross and others.

TALENTED AND POPULAR. Danny Kramer was a Boston man who began fighting in Vernon, Long Beach, San Diego, San Bernardino, Bakersfield and San Francisco during 1919-1920. In September of 1920, Kramer went to the east and began to carve out a name for himself. From this point on, he fought mostly in Philadelphia and on occasion returned to California for bouts in Los Angeles and Vernon. **(Courtesy Antiquities of the Prize Ring)**

HE DID IT ALL. Ben Whitman started as an amateur referee in New York and then officiated professional bouts, about eighty in all. Whitman came to California in 1919, opened a club in Santa Barbara and acted as manager, matchmaker and referee. Ben also promoted bouts in El Rio, Santa Maria and Inglewood. In 1925, he began refereeing bouts at Doyle's, Ascot and the Olympic Auditorium. Whitman was the third man in eight major world championship bouts held in the L.A. area from 1925-1946.

PROMISING START. Ernie Goozeman (Ernest Ghuzman) was from Arizona. He began boxing in Southern California in 1918-1921 and showed promise early on with victories over Eddie "Kid" Mende, Charley Roselli, Joe Miller, Al Walker, Young Farrell and Jimmy Brenton and draws with Danny Edwards, Al Walker and Tommy Cello. In 1921, he boxed in Australia and in 1923, he embarked on a tour to the Midwest United States and performed very well – winning a newspaper decision over Joey Sangor in Milwaukee after an apparent one-round knockout and capturing newspaper wins over Joe Burman, also in Milwaukee, and Jack Hausner in St. Louis. Goozeman stepped way up in competition in 1924 and engaged in competitive bouts with George Butch, Charles Ledoux, Joey Sangor, Eddie Shea and Pete Sarmiento. **(Courtesy Tom Scharf)**

A FAVORITE OF THE CROWD. Bert Colima (Ephraim Romero) was a darling of the four round bouts during 1919-1924. He engaged in many contests in Vernon, Los Angeles, Hollywood and elsewhere in California during these years. During his career, Colima gained victories over such men as Jackie Clark, Jimmy Delaney, Kid Mexico, "Sunny" Jim Williams, George Manley, Dave Shade, "Bermondsey" Billy Wells, Frank Farmer, Billy Shade, Ray Pelkey, Frankie Jones, "Tiger" Johnny Cline, Joe Roche, Hilario Martinez and Lew Chester.

HE STAYED OUTTA SIGHT AND LET 'EM FIGHT. Abe Roth was another outstanding referee during this period. Roth had a keen interest in boxing, being a former amateur boxer and a pretty good one. Abe was at home in the ring - calm, cool and collected at all times. He was a fine judge of boxing, rarely touched the fighters and stayed in the background. Roth was the referee in eight major world title bouts held in the LA area from 1931-1952.

IN HOLLYWOOD, WHO'S THE BOXER AND WHO'S THE ACTOR? Rudolph Valentino (left), actor turned boxer, throws a left at "Memphis" Gene Delmont (right) as Jack Dempsey, boxer turned actor, looks on. Valentino, famous film personality, appears to be in excellent shape. Dempsey, on the other hand, had only two official bouts from December 15, 1920 through July 3, 1923. The ring rust piled up.

A MARVELOUS COLLECTION OF BOXING FIGURES. Many famous old time boxing men showed up for a gathering on May 13, 1921 at Jack Doyle's Vernon Arena. Seated in the middle front (left to right) are Tod Sloan, the famous jockey, and Snowy Baker. Kneeling (left to right) are Jerry McCarthy, Jack Doyle, Ad Wolgast, Spike Robson, "Mexican" Joe Rivers, Sailor Petroskey and Charlie Murray. Standing (left to right) are Charlie O'Connor, Rube Smith, "Uncle" Tom McCarey, Megaphone Cook, Jack Jeffries, Willie Ritchie, Charles "Kid" McCoy, Jim Jeffries, Tom Sharkey, Jack Root, Billy Papke, Al Kaufmann, Tommy Ryan and Charles Eyton.

TALENTED BANTAM BATTLER. Georgie Marks was an outstanding fighter who was seen often in the Los Angeles area rings during 1917-1926. He twice captured the Bantamweight Championship of the Pacific Coast - in 1921 and 1926. His brother, Benny, was a top flyweight who had several famous battles with Fidel LaBarba as an amateur. During his career, Georgie gained victories over such men as Charlie "Kid" Moy, Young Farrell, Eddie "Kid" Mende, Danny Edwards, Ad Rubidoux, Frankie Dolan, "California" Joe Lynch, Dixie LaHood, Checkie Herman and Chuck Hellman.

THIS MAN GOT AROUND. M. L. Ruwin came to California in 1922, after years of officiating all over America. When he was a younger man, he fought as a featherweight boxer, having 74 bouts and winning 31 of those by knockout. During his career, Ruwin refereed under the New York and Nebraska Boxing Commissions and had a strong voice in promoting ten round bouts in California by speaking to all the clubs in which he officiated.

THE CHAMP DOES SOME SPARRING. Heavyweight Champ, Jack Dempsey, on the left, gets in a little sparring with movie actress Florence Lee, wife of his trainer, Teddy Hayes. Dempsey was in California working on a film during his 1921-1923 period of inactivity. The lack of ring work eventually took its toll and hastened the decline of the hard-hitting "Mauler."

COME ON, BERT. Local favorite, Bert Colima (on the left), tangled with Jimmy O'Hagan (right) twice during 1923 and came away without a win. On July 10, O'Hagan won a decision. Then, on September 3, they battled to a draw. **(Courtesy Antiquities of the Prize Ring)**

A TICKET TO THE FIGHTS. In late 1923, Doyle built a new arena that seated 7,000 fans. It was close by his old site. Weekly boxing cards were run that usually consisted of seven fights. A couple of years later, the capacity was increased to 8,500 seats.

SALVADORE TO FACE BENJAMIN

Lightweight Kings Battle in Wind-up at Vernon

———◆———

Midget Smith Will Take on Young Farrell Tonight

———◆———

Capacity Crowd Expected at Doyle's New Coliseum

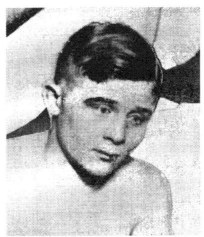

Midget Smith

With main event fighters sprinkled all over the program like freckles on Wes Barry's nose, Jack Doyle's brand new fight pavilion will be unveiled tonight. Something like ten thousand fans will be there in the hope that Jack will properly christen the arena by busting a bottle of champagne over Billy Coe's toupee.

Joe Benjamin, Phil Salvadore, Midget Smith—any one of them enough to fill Doyle's old pavilion—Young Farrell, one of the toughest banties ever developed out here, and a flock of other bouts to match will fill out the card although Jack's new place is so classy that probably not half of the crowd will get through gawking at it in time to look at the battlers in the earlier part of the nigh.

WILD WIND-UP

The wind-up bout between Benjamin and Salvadore ought to be the wildest thing in four-round history if advance indications are borne out. Benjamin, an extremely clever boxer from Jack Dempsey's camp and a hard hitter as well, meets in Salvadore a tough lightweight who has been a stumbling block to him and who has outpointed some of the best lightweights and welterweights that ever ventured into these parts.

Phil Salvadore

Jo Benjamin

BIG NIGHT IN VERNON ON AUGUST 28, 1923. Fans watched an excellent fight card of four round bouts, topped off by Joe Benjamin and Phil Salvadore battling to a close draw. Midget Smith decisively won over Young Farrell in a semi-windup contest. In other contests that night, Frankie Grandetta defeated Frankie Novey while draws resulted in contests between Kid Mexico and Midnight Edmundson, Packy McMullen and Joe White, Frankie Tierney and Johnny Adams, Louie Garcia and Johnny Reno.

Thousands Turned Away at Opening of Jack Doyle's New Arena

JACK DOYLE
Boxing Promoter at Vernon Arena, Los Angeles, Calif.

Some Features That Make Vernon Arena the Finest in World

Here are the salient facts about the new Doyle arena at Vernon, California, which had its premiere to a capacity crowd August 28th.

It was built in 35 days. The arena has a seating capacity of 9,000, of which 3,500 are reserved. There are 22 exits, 24 boxes and 8 loges. The cost was between $80,000 and $90,000.

It was designed and constructed by R. E. (Dick) Dusenberry.

The lobby encircles the entire reserved section, the interior being done in Tiffany colors and has indirect lighting.

The ring is lighted by 12 cinema spotlights, direct from the roof. Two huge fans in the roof provide ventilation.

Boxers enter the ring through the tunnel. Automatic seats are provided in corners of the ring. Running water is also provided for the ring.

The ring is equipped with an electric gong.

Front of building done in Egyptian stucco.

Every box in the arena is sold to prominent Los Angeles sportsmen and business firms, with the name of each on electric lighted name plates.

LOS ANGELES, CALIF.—More than 11,000 boxing fans attended the opening of Jack Doyle's new boxing arena at Vernon, August 28, when the greatest stadium in the West was thrown open to the public.

OPENING NIGHT AT DOYLE'S. Many fans were turned away on opening night, August 28, 1923, at Jack Doyle's new arena in Vernon. From the above article, it is seen that the facilities were first class.

THE O'DONNELL-BENJAMIN BOUT. Johnny O'Donnell (boxer on the left) beat Joe Benjamin (boxer to the right) in a sensational four-rounder at Jack Doyle's Vernon Arena on December 18, 1923. Key figures in the photograph - on the far left is Mike Collins (manager of O'Donnell, holding his coat), immediately behind O'Donnell is Stewart McLean (stablemate of O'Donnell), referee George Blake (partially blocked behind O'Donnell's head), and to the far right, in the bow tie, is Billy Bernstein (acting as manager of Benjamin in the place of Jack Kearns). Benjamin avenged this loss a month later in a bout also held in Vernon.

MANLEY-COLIMA. George Manley (left) beat Bert Colima in an upset in Hollywood on December 21, 1923. Key figures in the photograph - on the far left is Mike Collins (manager of Manley), in the center is referee George Blake (white shirt and bow tie), just behind Colima, on the right, is Dan Tobey (famous ring announcer) and on the far right in the white shirt is Dutch Meyers (manager of Colima).

HE HAD CONSIDERABLE INFLUENCE. Charley Keppen (far left photo) was a native Californian and one of the most popular men associated with athletics on the Pacific Coast. Keppen was director of the athletic activities for the Los Angeles Athletic Club from the teens into the twenties. He was also involved with various sporting events for all of California and the Pacific Coast, and many contests on the national level.

THE WINNER. In the near photo to the left, Keppen holds up the hand of a young boxer named Stevens, winner of the Olympics Lightweight Competition at the 1932 games in Los Angeles.

POPULAR LIGHTWEIGHT. Joe Benjamin was a popular lightweight who was active in the area in 1918 and again during the 1922-1925 years. Benjamin hailed from the San Francisco area and had boxed since 1915. He had appeared in such cities as Philadelphia, New York and Portland, Oregon. During his area appearances, he had more than 25 bouts. **(Courtesy Antiquities of the Prize Ring)**

PUT DOWN YOUR DUKES, BIG FELLA. In this tattered old photograph, Heavyweight Champion, Jack Dempsey (far left), squares off against giant John Aasen, all eight feet of him. In front, are Abe Gordon (left) and Young Nationalista (Federico Buenaflor), who battled each other at the Vernon Arena during April of 1924. Nationalista was a scrappy competitor who gained victories during his career over Frankie Grandetta (3 times), Georgie Rivers (twice), Tommy O'Brien (twice), "Jockey" Joe Dillon, "Memphis" Pal Moore, Abe Goldstein, Benny Schwartz, Bobby Garcia and Paul Medrano.

HE WAS THE MAIN MAN. Don J. Shields was the actual author of the bill permitting bouts of ten rounds or more. Shields did much leg work in promoting the bill to the people of California. He had numerous contacts, having been a resident since 1894, and had considerable experience as a boxing promoter. It was reported that he drove his own automobile over 30,000 miles in the effort to popularize the bill and obtain signatures.

HE HELPED MAKE THE CHANGE. In 1924, Senator Harry F. Morrison was the politician who promoted the bill to allow bouts of ten rounds or more to be held in California. The bill eventually passed due to a vote of the people. Fight clubs appeared immediately and prospered.

O'DONNELL-WELLS. On May 6, 1924 at the Vernon Arena, four sizzling rounds were fought by Johnny O'Donnell (left) and "Bermondsey" Billy Wells of Britain, in a bout that resulted in a "draw" decision. Key figures in the photograph - on the far left is Mike Collins (manager of O'Donnell), in the center is referee George Blake (the taller man in the center with white shirt and bow tie) and behind Wells, on the right, is Charley Harvey (manager of Wells).

SALVADORE AND HOPPE IN A DRAW

Lightweights Box Even in Main Event at Wilmington Arena Opening

FIGHT AT THE NEW WILMINGTON ARENA. On August 27, 1924, the new Wilmington Arena opened before 4,200 fans with Phil Salvatore fighting a draw with Dick Hoppe in the main event. Winners were Joe Medina over Jack Spencer, Pico Ramies over Georgie Etcell, Billy Hogan over Willie Singer and Billie Afoa over Frank Corbett by a knockout. Also, Georgie Lopez and Pedro Pablo battled to a draw as did Larry Murphy and Willie "Wildcat" O'Brien. Some 1,500 fans were turned away.

ALKIE AKOL. Akol, born in the Philippines, never fought there. He was a Champion in the United States Navy during World War I as an amateur. His professional career was less than sensational but he always gave an interesting performance. During his brief career, he defeated Frankie Grandetta twice, Frankie Novey, Pinky Urquidi, Benny Diaz, Roy "Kid" Riley, Pedro Villa and Angel De La Cruz.

CALIFORNIA MAY GET 10-ROUND BOXING LAW

Los Angeles, Calif.—The ten-round boxing bill sponsored by Don Shields of Sacramento stands an excellent chance of being passed at the November election, according to the belief of local boxing promoters. Los Angeles supported the initiative petition better than any other section of the State and an intensive campaign for the bill will be carried on here.

THE MOVE TOWARDS TEN-ROUNDERS. Here is an article, published in September of 1924, that announced the possibility of holding ten round boxing contests in California.

MEX KID AND HIS CRONIES. Kid Mexico (Todd Faulkner), center, is chatting with some old buddies, Charley Lacy (left) and Charlie Winninger (right). The Kid fought in the ring for sixteen years but was most active in the early to mid-1920s. A crafty boxer, he was probably at his best during 1924 when he racked up twelve victories. In addition to his fighting, Kid was actively promoting cards in Huntington Beach. **(Courtesy J.J. Johnston)**

THEY DIDN'T BELIEVE IT. On November 17, 1924 in Culver City, Tony Fuente (left) knocked out Fred Fulton in 35 seconds of round one. Following the shocker, fans showed their discontent with the result and rioted, throwing items into the ring. Fuente had a fine record with only four losses in nearly 40 bouts. Fulton, on the other hand, was a world famous fighter with over 80 wins to his credit, including official victories over many "name" heavyweights – Sam Langford, Carl Morris, Tom Cowler, Ed "Gunboat" Smith, "Fireman" Jim Flynn, Dan "Porky" Flynn, Arthur Pelkey, Bob Devere, Tom "Bearcat" McMahon and Frank Moran.

DIDN'T LIKE IT. The brief article excerpt to the right describes the fans' response to the 1924 Tony Fuente-Fred Fulton bout.

KNOCK-OUT IS GREETED BY SHOUTS OF "FAKE"

Bout Lasts Less Than One Minute; Fulton Hits the Canvas Three Times During Excitement

Tony Fuente, the so-called champion of Mexico, climbed another rung on the ladder to the top of the heavyweight heap by knocking out Fred Fulton, the Minnesota plasterer, in a little less than one minute of fighting in the Culver City American Legion arena last night. After Referee Earl Mohan had counted Fulton out the fans howled their disapproval, shouting "Fake!" and filling the ring with cushions.

TEDDY BOY. Teddy Silva fought about as many draws as he had wins or losses. In a career that lasted from the late teens through the late twenties, Silva held the Bantamweight Championship of the Pacific Coast and garnered victories over such men as Johnny Adams, Frankie Novey, "Dandy" Dick Griffin, Frankie Dolan, Young Nationalista, Young Farrell, Tommy Milton and Frankie Grandetta. Also, he had draws with Johnny Buff, Young Nationalista, Irving "Izzy" Glassier, Young Farrell, Georgie Marks, Ad Rubidoux, Vic Foley and Georgie Rivers.

HOLLYWOOD LEGION STADIUM. Above is a view of the first version of the Hollywood Legion Stadium, which had a capacity of about 4,500. Weekly boxing cards were started there in 1921 and were very popular. In 1938, it was torn down to make way for the second and final version of the famed boxing venue. **(Courtesy www.HollywoodPhotographs.com)**

SLICK WELTER. Harry Ritzer was a clever welterweight of the mid-1920s who fought primarily in Vernon, Hollywood, San Pedro and Wilmington. Harry claimed wins over George Gilmore, "Sailor" Billy Vincent, Mike Hector and Alex Trambitas. Also, he fought a ten-rounder with the great Jack Britton but came out on the short end of the decision.

TOM KENNEDY. Here, young Tom (on the left) poses with Joe Jeannette, a great black fighter of the teens. Joe tangled with Jack Johnson in the ring eight times. Kennedy was a "white hope" heavyweight, chasing after Johnson's title. He boxed during the teens and met the likes of Battling Levinsky, Frank Moran, Carl Morris and Al Palzer.

TAKE IT FROM ME, KID. The older Tom Kennedy, a few years later, is giving Hank Bath, young heavyweight contender, some pointers in a Los Angeles gym. Tom was matchmaker at the Hollywood Legion Stadium after his ring career ended. He was also involved in managing boxers and acting in movies.

FRANKIE BOY. Frankie Grandetta was a familiar face in area rings from 1923-1926. Afterwards, he fought elsewhere. Frankie was called the "Hollywood Sheik" because of his many appearances in the movie town. Grandetta built a nice record early in his career and during his tenure in the ring, he defeated such men as Abe Gordon, Irving "Izzy" Glassier, Frankie Novey, Benny Marks, Ernie Hood, Benny Furrell, "Sailor" Willie Gordon and Harvey Holiday. He also fought a draw with Billy Mascott and two draws with Frankie Dolan.

Chapter Four

The Ten-Round Era and Great Depression

1925-1942

There were major changes in California boxing with the advent of the **Ten-Round Law**. A state athletic commission was created to govern professional boxing and wrestling and some amateur boxing shows. There were three unsalaried members on this commission along with a salaried secretary and inspectors who were paid on a per show basis.

Professional bouts with a maximum number of ten rounds were allowed if a decision were rendered. Bouts with a maximum of twelve rounds were permitted if no decision were rendered. Legal control of professional boxing switched from the local level to the state level.

The **Ten-Round Law** mandated that state athletic commission expenses were paid by money from a tax of five percent of the gross receipts from the gates of shows in the state. If funds were left over after the payment of commission expenses, they went to pay for the construction of homes for veterans. With its implementation, the **Ten-Round Era** began.

Charitable or semi-charitable boxing venues such as the Hollywood Legion Stadium were exempt from the state tax. With Tom Gallery at the helm as a matchmaker and then as a matchmaker/manager, the Hollywood Legion Stadium continued to have much success throughout the late 1920s.

There was a tremendous amount of professional boxing in California by 1925. During the late 1920s, over one thousand professional boxing shows were staged in California on an annual basis. (Consider the fact that the United States averaged fewer than one thousand boxing shows per year during the 1990s and the first few years of the Twenty-first Century despite having a population of upwards towards three hundred million.)

At the beginning of 1925, the Los Angeles area had boxing shows every day of the week except Sunday. Cards were staged at the Assembly AC on Mondays, the Vernon Arena on Tuesdays, San Fernando and the Wilmington Bowl on Wednesdays, Pasadena and the Chief Petty Officers' Club in San Pedro on Thursdays, the Hollywood Legion Stadium on Fridays and the Lyceum on Saturdays. By the latter part of 1925, boxing shows at the Chief Petty Officer's Club, the Assembly AC, the Lyceum and the club in San Fernando all fell by the wayside.

After the boxing cards at the Lyceum ceased, promoter Dick Donald staged boxing cards on Saturdays on a large scale at the local automobile racing track, Ascot Park. Despite some large gates and crowds, Donald lost money and moved over to the new Wrigley Field with mixed success.

During January of 1925, ground was broken for construction of the fabled Olympic Auditorium on the southwest corner of Grand Avenue and West Eighteenth Street. World Heavyweight Champion, Jack Dempsey, and movie actress, Estelle Taylor, were present. Being the site of boxing shows up to the present day, the Olympic Auditorium went on to be the most famous boxing venue in Los Angeles. At the time it was built, with a capacity of 10,400, the Olympic Auditorium was lavishly furnished as compared to other boxing arenas in California and included plush seating fit for an opera house.

The Vernon Arena and the Olympic Auditorium were located within a few miles of each other. With boxing shows staged on a weekly basis at both venues, attendance was affected at both sites. Starting in 1926, due to a California Athletic Commission edict, the Vernon Arena and Olympic Auditorium staged boxing shows on alternating weeks.

The Olympic Auditorium was in receivership during the first year-and-a-half of existence before the Los Angeles Athletic Club (LAAC) and the Title Insurance and Trust Company got a court order to have the new arena turned over to them in early 1927. The LAAC was the owner of the Olympic Auditorium for many decades. An LAAC administrator, Frank Garbutt, played a key part in many of the decisions involving the famed arena from 1927 until well into the 1940s.

At the time the LAAC assumed control of the Olympic Auditorium in early 1927, Jack Doyle was losing money while staging boxing cards in Vernon. The LAAC wanted to stage professional boxing cards at the Olympic Auditorium weekly rather than every other week. To do this, the LAAC agreed to lease the site to Doyle. This led to the Vernon Arena shutting down. Another factor for the lease agreement was the considerable success that Doyle had in the past as a boxing promoter.

But, Doyle had a tough time staging cards at the Olympic Auditorium. Part of the reason was that Dick Donald staged cards at Wrigley Field at that time. Donald also had some boxing cards that did not draw well.

Two of Donald's promotions that featured Ace Hudkins drew very well at Wrigley Field in 1927. However, the debacle surrounding the aborted World Welterweight Championship bout between Joe Dundee, the champion, and Hudkins, the challenger, removed Donald from the promoting game later that year.

With Donald out of the picture, Doyle staged big boxing shows at Wrigley Field. He promoted the first two shows in California that drew gates of over $100,000 dollars. The first featured George Godfrey and Paolino Uzcudun in the main event in 1928. The other featured the second World Middleweight Title bout between Mickey Walker, the champion, and challenger Ace Hudkins, the following year.

In 1929, Doyle's boxing promotion grossed $695,000 in gate receipts, by far the largest of the "for profit" clubs in California. The Olympic Auditorium wrestling promoter, Lou Daro, grossed a total of $325,000 from his shows. The California State Athletic Commission received five percent in tax money from gate receipts of about 2.8 million dollars from wrestling and boxing shows staged under its auspices.

During the middle 1920s, the Hollywood Legion Stadium boxing cards made a profit of $75,000 per year despite the fact the arena had a capacity of only about 4,500. It remained the most successful and most stable boxing venue in California during both the 1920s and the 1930s.

There were new boxing clubs in the Los Angeles area that started up in the latter part of the 1920s. Two of the most notable clubs were the Main Street Athletic Club and the club in Ocean Park.

The Main Street Athletic Club staged weekly cards on Saturdays in 1926 with Carlo Curtis acting as the promoter. This club appealed to fans of Mexican descent. In the new local Spanish newspaper, *La Opinion,* there was considerable coverage of Main Street Athletic Club cards and the Mexican-American boxing hero, Bert Colima. The club operated on a weekly basis into the early 1930s.

Ocean Park was a boxing venue over a span of two decades. There was boxing on a weekly basis into the early 1930s.

During the late 1920s, with "Doc" Moffett and Morrie Cohen as the respective matchmakers, both the Wilmington Bowl and Pasadena continued as venues with boxing on a weekly basis. But, in December 1929, a fire destroyed the first version of the Wilmington Bowl. The second version of the Wilmington Bowl was a brick building that cost $50,000 and had a capacity of 3,500. It opened in June of 1930, with C.B. Glascock as the matchmaker and continued as a boxing venue into the 1950s.

With the occurrence of the **Great Depression**, professional boxing clubs in California were hit hard. Almost every club had difficulty. Many staged cards less often. At a number of venues, general admission prices were slashed from the usual price of one dollar in the 1920s to as little as twenty-five cents. Consequently, the average gate of shows was much lower during the 1930s. A number of the clubs staged amateur boxing cards under the control of the State Athletic Commission in an effort to attract boxing fans.

Another effect of the **Great Depression** was the rapid turnover of promoters and matchmakers, even at the most stable boxing venues. A number of best-known boxing men moved from job-to-job.

Promoters staged more professional wrestling shows in the 1930s than in the 1920s. Like all professional and some amateur boxing shows in California, all wrestling shows were under the control of the State Athletic Commission. Most professional wrestlers engaged in more bouts than the most active of boxers during a given year. They also experienced longer careers.

As things worsened, promoter Jack Doyle and his matchmaker, Hayden "Wad" Wadhams, had difficulty attracting fans to the Olympic Auditorium. By 1933, Doyle staged boxing just occasionally, rather than every week. According to the Los Angeles Times, Doyle lost $2,400 when he staged a boxing show at the Olympic. There were some shows where the attendance was only about 2,500, about twenty-five percent of the capacity of the famed arena.

When Doyle staged the World Welterweight Championship bout between Young Corbett and Jimmy McLarnin, at Wrigley Field on May 29, 1933, he reportedly lost $20,000. As a result of this promotional failure and the lack of success at the Olympic during the **Great Depression**, Wadhams resigned as matchmaker. Later, Doyle retired from promoting boxing cards. Reportedly, Doyle was doing well in the oil business at the same time he promoted boxing.

Even the highly successful Hollywood Legion Stadium encountered a rough time. The year 1931 was the worst and the manager/matchmaker, Tom Gallery, resigned in the latter part of the year. Gene Doyle and Charley MacDonald, a well-known manager of boxers, took over the duties as the manager and matchmaker, respectively. Doyle left the job less than two years later and MacDonald became manager while continuing to act as matchmaker.

After 1931, the Hollywood Legion Stadium rebounded quickly. A new arena was built, with a larger capacity than before, and while it was under construction, boxing cards under the auspices of the Hollywood Legion Post No. 43 were staged outdoors at Gilmore Stadium. On September 2, 1938, the new version of the Hollywood Legion Stadium offered its first card. The capacity of the new building was approximately 6,300, almost 2,000 more than the old arena. In the new arena, the Hollywood Legion Stadium boxing cards attracted capacity crowds well into the 1940s.

In 1940, black boxers participated in cards at the Hollywood Legion Stadium for the first time. Many "name" blacks fought there until the stadium shut down in 1959.

The struggle to stage shows at the Olympic Auditorium continued until 1943. A number of well-known boxing people made attempts with varying degrees of success, including Tom Gallery, Dick Donald, Joe Waterman, Stephen "Suey" Welch, Harry Popkin, Jimmy Murray, Joe Lynch and Reginald "Snowy" Baker.

A boxing man from the Northwest, Joe Waterman, was quite successful in several stints as matchmaker during a period spanning from 1935 to 1942. But, he was forced out in 1937 although he came back at least twice. One reason for the success of Waterman during his first stint, from 1935 to 1937, was that he slashed the ticket prices, notably general admission for regular boxing shows, down to twenty-five cents. The gate for a capacity crowd for a regular boxing show at the Olympic Auditorium was a little over $5,000 as compared $19,000 per gate during the late 1920s for the same type of show. Another reason for Waterman's success was that he found a large pool of talented boxers for his shows.

The **Great Depression** hit the smaller clubs in the Los Angeles area hard, too. After holding boxing cards less often than in better economic times, the Main Street Athletic Club and the Culver City Arena eventually shut down. Fewer professional boxing cards were staged in Wilmington, Pasadena and Ocean Park as well. With boxing men such as Joe Waterman and Harry Rudolph "Babe" McCoy having tenures as matchmakers, boxing in Ocean Park under Promoter Mike Hirsch made a dramatic comeback as the economy became better during the late 1930s and early 1940s.

THEY WERE IN CHARGE. George Blake (referee and fight manager, standing in the middle) is shown meeting with the first California State Athletic Commission. Members of the Commission, left to right, are Louis Almgren (standing), William Hanlon (seated), Blake (not a member), Walter Yarwood (seated; Secretary of the Commission but not a member) and Seth W.P. Strelinger (far right), Chairman of the Commission

GREAT BOXING SITE. Above is an interior view of the "first" Wilmington Bowl. The initial big fight card of 1925 at the Bowl had Buck Curtis versus Johnny "Young" Datto on January 7. The result of this bout was a "draw". The club ran continually until December 6, 1929 when a careless smoker set the place afire, causing damage that sidelined the club until June 4, 1930. It reopened at a cost of some $50,000 in repairs.

MATCHUP. Mickey Walker (left) and Bert Colima square off before their bout on February 24, 1925 at the Vernon Arena. Although Walker was Welterweight Champion of the World at this time, this was not a title fight. Colima held unequalled popularity with the local boxing fans. Heavyweight Champion Jack Dempsey is standing behind Walker. Referee Harry Lee is between the men. **(Courtesy Clay Moyle)**

HEY, YOU CAN'T HELP. On the right is a scene from the battle. Walker flattened Bert Colima (down) in his corner in round seven. Bert's manager, "Dutch" Meyers, can be seen (lower right corner) trying to get some smelling salts to his fighter. In spite of the fact that Colima was knocked out, the referee disqualified him because of Meyers' action. Nevertheless, some historians call this bout a knockout for Walker.

THE BOXING SKILLS MAN. George Blake was an all-around boxing man. He was one of the most famous referees from Southern California and an instructor at the Los Angeles Athletic Club where he developed many outstanding amateur boxers. Blake was also a clever manager and second. In addition, he was masterful at handling financial affairs for his boxers. Three talented fighters developed by Blake were Fidel LaBarba, Jackie Fields and Joe Salas. From 1933 to 1940, George refereed seven major world title bouts in the area. He also refereed a number of others across the country during his career.

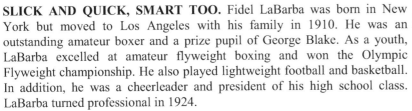

SLICK AND QUICK, SMART TOO. Fidel LaBarba was born in New York but moved to Los Angeles with his family in 1910. He was an outstanding amateur boxer and a prize pupil of George Blake. As a youth, LaBarba excelled at amateur flyweight boxing and won the Olympic Flyweight championship. He also played lightweight football and basketball. In addition, he was a cheerleader and president of his high school class. LaBarba turned professional in 1924.

EXCELLENT FIGHTER. Jackie Fields (Jacob Finkelstein) was born in Chicago but moved with his family to Los Angeles as a youngster. He was another star pupil of George Blake and won the Olympic Featherweight Gold Medal in 1924. Fields turned pro soon afterwards and was unbeaten with only one draw at the time he lost to Jimmy McLarnin on November 12, 1925 in Los Angeles. On March 25, 1929, Fields defeated "Young" Jack Thompson in ten rounds in Chicago to capture the NBA Welterweight title. Four months later, he won from Joe Dundee on a second round foul in Detroit in another NBA Welterweight Championship contest.

BRAINY GUY. Pasadena's Morrie Cohen, perhaps the youngest promoter in California boxing lore, was applauded as early as 1925 by DeWitt Van Court. Morrie had the old Armory on Union Street in Pasadena and showed weekly cards for years. He took a hiatus when the depression set in but came back time and again in the face of real stiff competition. A rather private sort, Cohen shunned the spotlight, took care of business and led by example. He was said to have been a very good artist. It was Morrie who gave Jackie Fields his first feature bout early in 1925. The Armory was one of the few small clubs that sold out frequently in the late 1920s. Cohen is also credited with giving black fighters a boost in the Los Angeles area.

CHAMP TURNED BUSINESSMAN. Jack Root, on the right, was the first manager of the Olympic Auditorium. At one time during his life, Root was a classy boxer who was the first to hold the Light-Heavyweight Championship of the World. Following his boxing days, he got into other ventures. Managing the Olympic was a work of passion for him. Shown here, he is shaking hands with Jack Dempsey, the great heavyweight champion. Dempsey never fought at the famed arena although he acted as referee there. **(Courtesy Antiquities of the Prize Ring)**

COSTLY MOVE. "Doc" Moffett was the matchmaker in Wilmington from 1924-1929 and staged boxing shows on a regular basis. He left Wilmington shortly after the fire ruined the "first" version in 1929. Bill Yeager took over.

GRAND OLD PLACE. The Olympic Auditorium opened on August 5, 1925 and was the site for many world famous entertainers as well as top flight boxing and wrestling talent. Among the actors and actresses who appeared here were Mae West, Lupe Velez, Ruby Keeler, Al Jolson, Robert Taylor and Barbara Stanwyck, to list a few. Some name people in boxing who competed here were Enrique Bolanos, John Thomas, Fidel LaBarba, Ace Hudkins, Raul Rojas and "Mando" Ramos. Wrestlers like Jim Londos, "Dynamite" Gus Sonnenberg, the "Mighty" Hans Kampfer, Sandor Szabo and Joe Savoldi grappled here

A FAVORITE FIGHTER. Here, "Mushy" Callahan (Vincent Morris Scheer), on the right, shakes hands with Young "Baby" Manuel. The man in the middle is unidentified. On August 18, 1925 in Vernon, Callahan defeated James "Red" Herring in ten rounds and laid a "claim" to the Junior Welterweight Championship of the World. On September 21, 1926 in Vernon, he defeated Myron "Pinkey" Mitchell for the NBA Junior Welterweight crown. Callahan won two title defenses in 1927 outside of California and was at the Olympic Auditorium on May 28, 1929, when he knocked out Fred "Dummy" Mahan in three rounds to retain the title. "Mushy" lost his title to Jackie "Kid" Berg in London on February 18, 1930, when he was stopped in ten rounds. **(Courtesy Antiquities of the Prize Ring)**

DOYLE WILLING TO CHANGE BACK. In this clipping, by late 1925, Jack Doyle had decided to switch back to the four rounders for his boxing cards due to his excessive loss of money.

> Mark Kelly, conductor of a feature column in the Los Angeles Examiner, writes as follows:
>
> "Jack Doyle's decision to go back to the old four-round fights and to discontinue big guarantees to fighters comes as no surprise to close followers of the local situation. Doyle has had no success worth mentioning since the return of legalized boxing.
>
> Truth is that Doyle has dropped more than $30,000 under legalized boxing. He made much more than that in the old four-round days.
>
> * * *
>
> Doyle is finding out that there are too many fights being fed to the public. Somebody's got to suffer, and to date it appears that Doyle is carrying the load. On the other hand, the new Olympic Club has not been any sensational boxing success.
>
> The public is cooling off in its enthusiasm.
>
> Two good fight cards a week are sufficient. Any more than that is putting too great a strain on traffic.
>
> Doyle reduces prices and restores four-round boxing. That may help some. But Doyle is not abandoning his boxing promotion—merely gearing his gait to the road he travels. When big attractions bob up Doyle will resume big promotion, but as a weekly dish big bouts are not only hard to get, but harder to sell to the public.

WORLD CHAMP. On December 2, 1925, Tod Morgan (Albert Morgan Pilkington), on the left, stopped Mike Ballerino (right) in ten rounds at the Olympic Auditorium to capture the Junior Lightweight Championship of the World. Morgan was busy in 1926, defending his Junior Lightweight crown four times. He knocked out Kid Sullivan in six rounds and won decision victories over Joe Glick, Johnny Dundee and Carl Duane. In 1927, he scored two more title wins when he defeated Vic Foley in twelve rounds and beat Joe Glick on a foul in round fourteen

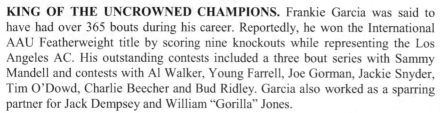

KING OF THE UNCROWNED CHAMPIONS. Frankie Garcia was said to have had over 365 bouts during his career. Reportedly, he won the International AAU Featherweight title by scoring nine knockouts while representing the Los Angeles AC. His outstanding contests included a three bout series with Sammy Mandell and contests with Al Walker, Young Farrell, Joe Gorman, Jackie Snyder, Tim O'Dowd, Charlie Beecher and Bud Ridley. Garcia also worked as a sparring partner for Jack Dempsey and William "Gorilla" Jones.

HERE'S HOW IT'S DONE, BIG FELLOW. Phil Salvadore (Philip Joseph Michell), right, spars with actor Ken Harlan on the set of the 1926 film, *Twinkletoes*. His brother, Sally Salvadore, was also a boxer. Phil had hot hands during 1919-1920 and racked up many victories. Over his career, he had wins against such men as Kid Mexico, Dave Shade, "Mexican" Joe Rivers, Jimmy Finley, Basil Galiano, Joe Benjamin, Dick Hoppe, Vincent "Pepper" Martin and Sammy Mandell. **(Courtesy Antiquities of the Prize Ring)**

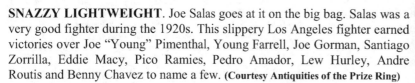

SNAZZY LIGHTWEIGHT. Joe Salas goes at it on the big bag. Salas was a very good fighter during the 1920s. This slippery Los Angeles fighter earned victories over Joe "Young" Pimenthal, Young Farrell, Joe Gorman, Santiago Zorrilla, Eddie Macy, Pico Ramies, Pedro Amador, Lew Hurley, Andre Routis and Benny Chavez to name a few. **(Courtesy Antiquities of the Prize Ring)**

ANOTHER LIGHT ONE. Ad Cadena was a top L.A. fighter during his career, from 1924-1933. In his very first fight, he defeated Young Corbett III. Later, he added to his list of conquests such men as Eddie Sylvester, Young Brown, Sailor Ashmore, Joe Brown, Ernie Goozeman, Jimmy Hackley, Jack Sparr, Pedro Amador and Nick Antonio.

TOUGH JOHNNY. Johnny Adams, shown with manager Tom Jones, fought from 1920-1931, won nearly 80 bouts, and was Lightweight Champion of the Pacific Coast in 1924. Among those he defeated during his career were Irving "Izzy" Glassier, Ad Rubidoux, Mushy Callahan, Johnny Lamar, "Oakland" Frankie Burns, Johnny Trambitas, Phil Salvadore, Ace Hudkins, Tommy O'Brien and Dick Hoppe. **(Courtesy Antiquities of the Prize Ring)**

A WILLING SCRAPPER. Eddie Huffman (sitting) was born in Mississippi and began his boxing career in California rings in 1923. A feisty fellow, Eddie boxed often in Wilmington, Vernon and Los Angeles. His career peaked during 1924-1925. He earned wins over Tony Fuente, Floyd Johnson, Bert Colima, Jack DeMave, Bob Roper, Pat McCarthy and Tony "Young" Marullo during his ring tenure. Following a loss to Leo Mitchell in 1928, Eddie retired from the ring. Here, Eddie is shown with his handlers. **(Courtesy Antiquities of the Prize Ring)**

GOOD MATCHMAKER. Joe Levy was one of the most prominent boxing men in Los Angeles over a span of several decades. As a manager, Levy piloted "Mexican" Joe Rivers, who was in his peak years at the time. Levy went on to be a matchmaker, serving at the Olympic Auditorium in Los Angeles, at the Dreamland Arena in San Francisco and in Portland. During his first stint at the Olympic Auditorium, Levy had a great deal of success, generating a profit of $35,000 despite staging shows on alternating weeks in 1926. In the 1930s, Levy was a promoter, using Gilmore Stadium as a venue.

A BUSY FELLOW. Pedro Amador had nearly 50 fights between 1926 and 1929, won the Super Featherweight Championship of Panama in 1927 and fought often in the Los Angeles area. Among those he defeated during his career were Toby Montoya, Jake "Kid" Sherman, Johnny Lamar, Ernie Goozeman, Earl Force, Jose Lombardo and Ritchie "Sailor" King. He also had draws with Joe Salas, "Doc" Snell and Billy Townsend. **(Courtesy Antiquities of the Prize Ring)**

A BIG, STRONG MAN. Heavyweight Neil Clisby fought primarily in Southern California from 1923-1930. During his career, Clisby defeated such men as Vic Alexander, "Chief" John Metoquah, "Wild" Bill Cusick, Tony Fuente, Bob Lawson, Mack House, John Lester Johnson, "Long" Tom Hawkins, Dynamite Jackson, "Young" Bob Fitzsimmons and Tony Galento. On July 5, 1927, Clisby met big George Godfrey but lost in seven rounds. His most famous fight was a loss against Primo Carnera in 1930. **(Courtesy Antiquities of the Prize Ring)**

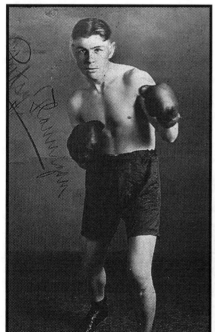

PATSY FROM VALLEJO. Patsy Flannigan was a lightweight who fought often in Los Angeles, Hollywood and Pasadena during the 1922-1933 years. His major wins came against George Spencer, Weldon "Tuffy" Wing, Buddy Ryan and Ralph Lincoln.

WINNING THE TITLE. The fighter from Los Angeles, Fidel LaBarba (standing), won the World Flyweight Championship on January 21, 1927 at New York's Madison Square Garden when he defeated Elky Clark in twelve rounds. Here, Clark is shown down in the first round. The referee is Patsy Haley.

BIG, SUPER STRONG AND POWERFUL. George Godfrey hailed from Mobile, Alabama but was a popular heavyweight on the national scene. Godfrey appeared in the Los Angeles area several times during 1925-1927 and won eleven contests here during those years. Many people thought he was among the best big men in the world during the late 1920s, perhaps the very best.

BABY TEACHES KIDS. "Baby" Sal Sorio (Gaspar Holguin Soria), right, seen with some children, waged ring wars from 1925-1935. Winner of nearly 70 bouts, he defeated such men as Al Walker, Dixie LaHood, Johnny McCoy, Mushy Callahan, Sammy Brown, Homer Gaines and Mickey Cohen. **(Courtesy Antiquities of the Prize Ring)**

HE'S UP TO SOMETHING. Dick Donald (center) explains to Bud Taylor (left) and his manager, Eddie Long (right) just how much money they can make by letting him promote a fight in Los Angeles.

TAKE THAT, SARGE. Ace Hudkins (left), the "Nebraska Wildcat," has just knocked down "Sergeant" Sammy Baker in their July 25, 1927 contest at Wrigley Field. Hudkins won a ten round decision, avenging an earlier knockout loss to Baker in New York. On February 17, 1928, Hudkins defeated Baker again in ten rounds, this time in New York. Hudkins was an aggressive fighter who fought from the lightweight through the light-heavyweight classes and even went on to win the Heavyweight Championship of California in 1931.

AT THE BARON'S. Baron Von Stumme was a Los Angeles promoter and manager during the 1920s. Shown here is the Baron, on the far left, checking out two of his boxers, Earl Caustin and Lew Sarver. On the far right is trainer Dave Landau.

FATHER OF FILIPINO BOXING. Frank Churchill operated out of New York and then shifted his base to Chicago and Los Angeles. He also promoted boxing shows in the Philippines and was fundamental in bringing the Filipino fighters to America. During his career as a manager, he managed many top fighters, including World Champions Pancho Villa, Tod Morgan and Mike Ballerino. Churchill also managed Speedy Dado, recognized as Bantamweight Champion of the World in the state of California. In addition, he managed Pete Sarmiento and Clever Sencio.

DID NOT FIGHT. Joe Dundee (right) and his manager, Max Waxman, appeared in a Los Angeles court in 1927 on a charge of false advertisement. An October, 1927 title bout for Dundee, the Welterweight Champion, against Ace Hudkins was postponed due to the threat of rain. When an attempt was made to schedule the contest on a date in November, Dundee, whose real name was Samuel Lazzaro, was not convinced he would receive the money he was seeking and refused to go through with the bout. Promoter Dick Donald ran into trouble with California authorities when the bout fell through.

GOLDIE. William "Goldie" Hess, born in Santa Monica, was a very good fighter during his short career. He was unbeaten in 1926 and 1928 and had good years in 1927 and 1929. During his ring days, he beat such men as Ralph Lincoln, Billy Hart, Joe "Young" Pimenthal, Santiago Zorrilla, Tod Morgan, Leslie "Wildcat" Carter, "Baby" Sal Sorio, Eddie Thomas, Johnny Lamar, Ritchie "Sailor" King and Tommy Grogan. In 1931, he fought Jackie Berg, reportedly for the NBA Junior Welterweight title, but lost.

PACIFIC COAST CHAMP. Above, Ramon Montoya was a popular fighter during 1929-1931 in Hollywood and Los Angeles. At one time, Montoya claimed the Bantamweight Championship of the Pacific Coast. During his career, he earned victories over Young Nationalista, Albert "Chalky" Wright and Santiago Zorrilla and boxed two exciting "draw" contests - against Zorrilla and Kid Francis.

LET'S HAVE A LITTLE FUN. Newsboy Brown (David Montrose) was a top fighter in his class and won the Flyweight Championship of the World (as recognized by California) on January 3, 1928 at the Olympic Auditorium when he defeated Johnny McCoy in ten rounds. To the right, movie star Tom Mix (on the ladder) gets some sparring tips from the Newsboy while climbing down a ladder. Mix was a favorite actor in western movies and a real-life friend of Wyatt Earp, the Marshal of Wild West fame. **(Courtesy Antiquities of the Prize Ring)**

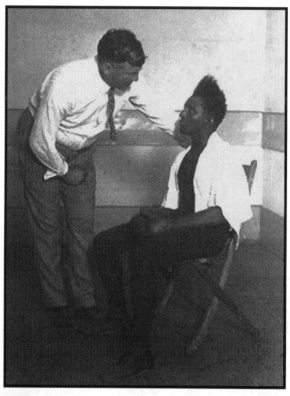

SAMPSON'S SCRAPPERS. The appearance of Filipino fighters in California increased interest in the sport and provided fans with some outstanding fisticuffs. Johnny Sampson was a well-known manager of Filipino fighters. Seen here (left to right) are Felix Villamore, Sampson, Young Nationalista and Young Datto, who later fought out of Cleveland as Johnny Datto.

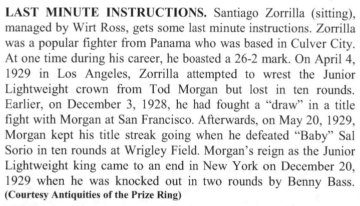

LAST MINUTE INSTRUCTIONS. Santiago Zorrilla (sitting), managed by Wirt Ross, gets some last minute instructions. Zorrilla was a popular fighter from Panama who was based in Culver City. At one time during his career, he boasted a 26-2 mark. On April 4, 1929 in Los Angeles, Zorrilla attempted to wrest the Junior Lightweight crown from Tod Morgan but lost in ten rounds. Earlier, on December 3, 1928, he had fought a "draw" in a title fight with Morgan at San Francisco. Afterwards, on May 20, 1929, Morgan kept his title streak going when he defeated "Baby" Sal Sorio in ten rounds at Wrigley Field. Morgan's reign as the Junior Lightweight king came to an end in New York on December 20, 1929 when he was knocked out in two rounds by Benny Bass. **(Courtesy Antiquities of the Prize Ring)**

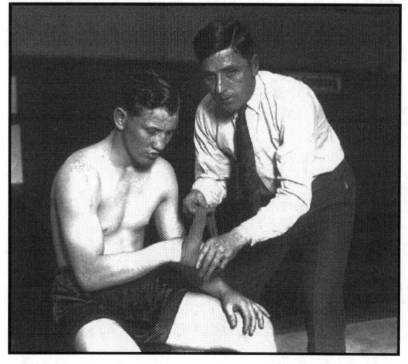

NEBRASKA WILDCAT. On October 29, 1929, Ace Hudkins sought to avenge an earlier loss to Mickey Walker. The "Toy Bulldog" had won a ten round decision over the "Ace" in Chicago on June 21, 1928 for the Middleweight Championship. But, Hudkins fared no better in this go and Walker retained his crown in ten rounds at Wrigley Field. During his career, Hudkins was a popular fighter in California, fighting primarily in Los Angeles and Hollywood. Shown here, Ace (sitting) is getting his hands wrapped by his brother, Clyde, who managed Ace and also "Young" Jack Thompson. **(Courtesy Antiquities of the Prize Ring)**

YOUNG JACK THOMPSON. Cecil Lewis Thompson (standing) was Los Angeles born and did his boxing primarily in California from 1922 until 1928, when he began to travel nationwide. "Young" Jack's career started to take off in 1926 when he had twenty-one fights and lost only three. Continually improving over the next three years, Thompson met Jackie Fields for the NBA Welterweight title in 1929, but lost. Nearly fourteen months later, on May 9, 1930, he took the title from Fields in Detroit in fifteen rounds. Then, Thompson lost his title to Tommy Freeman in Cleveland on September 5 but regained it on April 14, 1931 when he stopped Freeman in twelve rounds, also in Cleveland. Jack lost the crown for keeps to Lou Brouillard in fifteen rounds in Boston on October 23, 1931.

EXPLOSIVE GUY. Dynamite Jackson (on the left) talks with his trainer, Art Craig. Jackson fought Les Kennedy for the Heavyweight Championship of California on June 23, 1931 and scored a four round stoppage to capture the title. Jackson lost his California Heavyweight title to Ace Hudkins on September 15, 1931 in ten rounds and was stopped in eight rounds in an attempt to regain it against Tom Patrick on June 21, 1932.

TOUGH CUSTOMER. Tom Patrick was a Los Angeles native and a natural light heavyweight. He began boxing in 1926 and had an up-and-down career that peaked during 1931-1932. From early 1931 until early January of 1933, Patrick posted a 14-3 record and defeated some talented big men including Jimmy Hanna, Hans Birkie, Harry Thomas, Baxter Calmes (twice) and future Heavyweight Champion, Jim Braddock.

SOME GOOD IDEAS, PLEASE. Les Kennedy (left) gets some advice from the former heavyweight champion, Jim Jeffries. Kennedy built up a nice 29-5 record going into a rubber match with Dynamite Jackson on June 23, 1931 for the Heavyweight Championship of California. Kennedy lost this contest but during his time in the ring garnered victories over such men as Ernie Owens, John Lester Johnson, Meyer "K.O." Christner, Jack DeMave, Max Baer, Dynamite Jackson, Jack Van Noy, Baxter Calmes, Bob Godwin, Donald "Red" Barry, Stanley Poreda, Larry "Big Boy" Rawson and Enzo Fiermonte.

THE GREAT TONY. Here, Tony Canzoneri gets ready to take a swipe at a pitch. Canzoneri had a wonderful career as a top rated fighter in several weight classes and held championships in the Featherweight, Lightweight and Junior Welterweight classes. He is often ranked among the greatest all-time performers in the various divisions. Hailing from Louisiana, he boxed mostly in Brooklyn and New York as well as other large cities in the east. In a one year period, from November 1930 to November 1931, Tony engaged in six title bouts in two weight classes. Among these was the July 13, 1931 Junior Welterweight title bout at Wrigley Field, when Tony defeated Cecil Payne in ten rounds to retain his crown. In California bouts, dating from 1931 to 1939, he posted a 6-0 record. In addition to his victory over Payne, Canzoneri defeated Alberto "Baby" Arizmendi and Bobby Pacho in Los Angeles, Frankie Klick and Joe Gavras in San Francisco and Everett Simington in San Jose. **(Courtesy Antiquities of the Prize Ring)**

FLASHY GUY. Speedy Dado (Diosdado Posadas, left), shown with Gene Espinosa, was a colorful and popular fighter during the mid-1920s and throughout the 1930s. Dado was managed by Frank Churchill and was well known as a "clothes horse" with a flashy lifestyle. During his career, he defeated such men as Newsboy Brown, Benny Schwartz, Alberto "Baby" Arizmendi, Ernie Hood, "Panama" Al Brown, Eugene Huat, Joe Tei Ken, Hubert "Baby" Palmore, Abie Israel, Augie Curtis, Young Tommy and Lou Salica. After his fighting days, Speedy could be seen selling the *Knockout* programs outside the Olympic Auditorium on fight nights. **(Courtesy Antiquities of the Prize Ring)**

HE KNEW HIS BUSINESS. Joe Waterman promoted cards at the Olympic Auditorium during the 1930s and was well-known for his matchmaking. He was called "the best of them all" by many. He acted as referee in bouts in the Philippines while serving in the navy. Waterman spoke highly of the gameness of Filipino fighters.

THE MAGNIFICENT MILLERS. The talented trio of Abie, Benny and Hymie Miller fought out of Los Angeles from the mid 1920s until the mid 1930s. Abie (on the left) held the Welterweight Championship of California in 1936-1937. Benny, in the middle, was a clever boxing middleweight and light heavyweight and won a number of victories over some top men. Hymie, right, who won the National Amateur Flyweight Championship in his career, fought as a featherweight and lightweight and had wins over Don Kennedy, Johnny Gonzales, Benny Garcia and Charlie Miller (no relation) in his career. **(Courtesy Antiquities of the Prize Ring)**

THE BARN. Jim Jeffries owned property in Burbank at the corner of Victory Boulevard and Buena Vista Avenue. A building known as Jeffries Barn was located on this property and was a show place for amateur boxing. Contests were held on Thursday evenings from 1931 until 1953, when Jeffries passed away. A motion picture, *They Made Me A Criminal*, was filmed there and involved actor John Garfield in a boxing scene. After Jeffries' death, the barn was moved to the Knott's Berry Farm amusement park in Orange County.

GIMME DAT HAT. Sandy Garrison Casanova sits atop a motorcycle and gets the attention of his dog in this late-1920s photo. Garrison, who began fighting in the mid-1920s, had built an impressive record by 1932 and won the Heavyweight Championship of Mexico during that year. Sandy had an excellent career. Some of the men he defeated were Virgil "Lefty" Cooper, Lee Ramage, Ray Pelkey, Les Kennedy, Goyito Rico, Jimmy Hanna and Tony Poloni. **(Courtesy Antiquities of the Prize Ring)**

LEARNING THE TRADE. From July 30 through August 14 of 1932, the Olympic games were held in Los Angeles. Gold Medal winners in the various boxing weight classes were Istvan Enekes (Hungary), Flyweight; Horace Gwynne (Canada), Bantamweight; Carmelo Ambrosio Robledo (Argentina), Featherweight; Lawrence Stevens (South Africa), Lightweight; Edward Flynn (USA), Welterweight; Carmen Barth (USA), Middleweight; David Carstens (South Africa), Light Heavyweight; Santiago Lovell (Argentina), Heavyweight. Shown here is a ticket to the August 10 boxing events of the Tenth Olympiad.

THE K.O. MAN. Wesley "K.O." Ketchell (Wesley Hobbs Jr.) hailed from Utah and began his career in 1920. While traveling about, showing off his fists, he frequently appeared in California. Ketchell hit his stride during 1931-1933 and captured the Light Heavyweight Championship of the Pacific Coast with a victory over Ace Hudkins in 1932. A skilled craftsman and a very hard hitter, Ketchell defeated such men as "Oakland" Billy Harms, Billy Blake, Jock Malone, Al Webster, Pete Meyers, Young Firpo, Pete Cerkan, Herman Ratzlaff, Jimmy Hanna, Joe Cardoza, Benny Miller, Sandy Garrison Casanova, Ace Hudkins, Frank Rowsey, Tom Patrick, George Manley, Fred Lenhart and Bob Godwin during his tenure in the ring. **(Courtesy William Schutte)**

WORLD TRAVELER. On February 28, 1933 at the Olympic Auditorium, Freddie Miller, NBA Featherweight Champion, defeated Alberto "Baby" Arizmendi in ten rounds for the NBA crown. Three weeks later, on March 21 at the Olympic, Miller defeated Speedy Dado in ten rounds to retain his title. Miller won more than 200 contests during his career and was a true world traveler. He defended his title in England and boxed other contests in Wales, Scotland, Spain, France, Belgium, Ireland, Cuba, Canada, Mexico, South Africa and Venezuela. **(Courtesy Antiquities of the Prize Ring)**

WOW, LOOK AT THAT MITT. Here, Miller (center, left) shows his left hand to Young Tommy, Danny Kronenberg, Harry Gordon, Sammy Goldman and others.

FOUGHT THE BEST. Frank Rowsey was a scrappy light heavyweight who fought out of the area, primarily during the 1930s. A tough competitor, Rowsey tangled with the best in the world and managed tremendous wins against such men as Harold "Dutch" Weimer, Billy Papke Jr., Vearl Whitehead, Joe Vargas, Wesley "K.O." Ketchell, Fred Lenhart, Tony Poloni, Johnny Paychek, Charley "Killer" Coates and Paul Hartnek.

CHURCHILL PASSES. Frank Churchill passed away in his sleep on March 29, 1933 at his La Habra ranch. He was a shrewd manager yet had a benevolent way towards others.

JIMMY WINS A QUICKIE. Above, Jimmy McLarnin (on the left) won the Welterweight Championship of the World by stopping Young Corbett III (Raffaele Giordano, right) in one round at Wrigley Field on May 29, 1933. Following this bout, McLarnin had his hard fought three-bout series with Barney Ross. Then, he split a two-bout sequence with Tony Canzoneri and defeated Lou Ambers. After this bout, Corbett went on to post a 20-3 mark that included wins over Mickey Walker, Gus Lesnevich, Billy Conn, Fred Apostoli, Jackie Burke, Frankie Britt and Glen Lee. He lost only to Lou Brouillard, Conn and Apostoli.

FRANK CHURCHILL MOURNED

World-Famous Manager of Fighters Dies in His Sleep at La Habra; Made Champion of Villa and Searched in Vain for Another Star

BY PAUL LOWRY

Frank Churchill died in his sleep Wednesday night—died without seeing his dreams fulfilled of a Filipino fighter to take Pancho Villa's place.

One of the boxing world's greatest managers, Churchill had lived on his La Habra ranch in seclusion 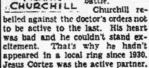 for the past three years. Quietly, unostentatiously, away from the "mob" that he loved so well, he continued to pull the strings that sent Speedy Dado, recognized in this State as the world's bantamweight champion, into battle.

Churchill rebelled against the doctor's orders not to be active to the last. His heart was bad and he couldn't stand excitement. That's why he hadn't appeared in a local ring since 1930. Jesus Cortez was the active partner.

KNEW DEATH WAS NEAR

The other night the lights went out for Churchill. The gong struck "ten." He knew it was coming. Had known it for a long time. But he faced the inevitable unflinchingly. He was a fighter.

He left this mortal world at the end of 59 years with only one remorse. He had never been able to develop a fighter to step into the shoes of the great little Pancho Villa, world's flyweight champion when he died in 1925.

A soldier of fortune with Rex Beach, Sid Grauman and Tex Rickard in the Yukon in the late '90's, Churchill gravitated to the Philippines in the early part of this century. He became a customs clerk.

Presently he became interested in fighting, and eventually built a fight palace that made him rich. There he discovered Villa. He brought him to the United States in 1932 and crowned him flyweight champion of the world.

He always said Villa was the greatest bundle of fighting machinery he ever saw. When Villa died as the result of an infected tooth after a fight with Jimmy McLarnin at San Francisco in 1925, Churchill was broken-hearted.

LOVED VILLA

He loved Villa like a son. He was never the same after the tiny fellow's death. When Churchill built his ranch mansion at La Habra he created a little "dream house" across the way. On the walls hung Villa's gloves. Pictures of his ring triumphs. The champion in dozens of poses.

Churchill was the father of Filipino boxing. He had many fine Filipino fighters. There was Dencio Pete Sarmiento and others. But he chased the elusive rainbow of another Villa.

A year after Villa's death Churchill believed he was well on his way to seeing his dream come true. He brought Clever Sencio to the States. Sencio made his maiden fights in this city. He was a riot. The boy was taken east and died after a fight with Bud Taylor in Milwaukee.

That was Frank Churchill's second heartbreak.

The third and final was when Speedy Dado failed to measure up to expectations. Speedy, a flashy little fellow, was never a Villa. He was something of an in and outer —a world beater one night and ordinary when great things were expected of him.

Churchill was one of the shrewdest managers the fight game ever saw. But he had a heart of gold. His benefactions to the unfortunates in the world he loved were many. But they were kept to himself.

He managed three world champions—Mike Ballerino and Tod Morgan, both junior lightweight kings, and Villa. He died as he lived, quietly and peacefully. And the fight world will mourn him long.

NO ONE KICKED THESE GUYS OUT. In 1933, some big name heavyweights gathered on the set during the filming of the movie, *The Prizefighter And The Lady*. From left to right are Jess Willard, Max Baer, W.S. Van Dyke (Film Director), Jim Jeffries, Jack Dempsey and Primo Carnera.

THE SLUGGER FROM THE MIDWEST. Ellsworth "Hank" Hankinson was born in Ohio and began his fighting there in late 1931. After a good year in 1932, followed by a year layoff, he migrated to California in 1934 and fought regularly in San Diego, Los Angeles and Hollywood. At one point, he had a 22-2-1 record in the Golden State. Hankinson was nearly 6-4 in height and usually weighed a little more than 210 pounds. He carried a stiff punch and during his career earned wins over such men as "Big" Sid Terris, Jack Van Noy, Hans Birkie, Fred Feary, Charley Retzlaff, Ford Smith, Donald "Red" Barry, Maxie Rosenbloom, Charley Massera, Alfred "Butch" Rogers, Lee Savold and George Godfrey. Most of these wins came in California rings. Here, Hank enjoys holding a puppy in his pocket. **(Courtesy Antiquities of the Prize Ring)**

READY BATTLER. Joe Cardoza (center, left) receives an award for one of his many victories. From 1926-1935, Joe appeared many times in Los Angeles, Hollywood, Culver City, Pasadena, San Bernardino and Wilmington. On this particular night, Joe defeated the Middleweight Champion of the United States Navy. In more than 100 battles in the ring, Cardoza defeated such men as Tony Azevedo, Bobby Bridges, Manuel Vasquez, Pete Meyers, Paul Delaney, Chick Roach, Billy Blake, Eddie "K.O." Roberts, Ace Conlon, Leo "Deacon" Kelly, Oscar Rankin and Hans Birkie. His pretty wife, Delia, is standing next to him (to the left). **(Courtesy Joe Cardoza Jr.)**

BRING IT ON, BOBBY. Bobby Pacho was a feisty competitor who performed often in Los Angeles and Hollywood during his early career. On March 27, 1934, Pacho met Champion Barney Ross for the Junior Welterweight Championship at the Olympic Auditorium. Ross won a ten round decision to retain his crown. The two men fought for the title again on December 10, 1934 in Cleveland and Ross won in twelve rounds. During his career, Pacho defeated such men as Tod Morgan, "Doc" Snell, Kenny LaSalle, Tony Falco, Eddie Ran, Salvy Saban, Leonard Del Genio, Cleto Locatelli, Glen Lee, William "Goldie" Hess and George Daly. Shown here, Bobby is explaining the use of gloves to some youngsters. **(Courtesy Antiquities of the Prize Ring)**

HOLLYWOOD LEGION STADIUM BOXING PROGRAM. Shown here is the front of the program for the August 24, 1934 boxing card. A number of bouts were scheduled but the main attraction for the evening was a bout between Georgie Hansford and Tommy Paul. Paul came into the bout with nearly 75 victories to his credit. Hansford had over 40 wins. The contest came to an end in the fourth round when Hansford won by a knockout.

AMONG THE BEST. Alberto "Baby" Arizmendi (on the left) began fighting in 1927 and engaged in ring battles for fifteen years. Fighting during a time when there were outstanding featherweights and lightweights, he posted a splendid record. "Baby" defeated such men as Fidel LaBarba, Speedy Dado, Young Tommy, Newsboy Brown, Archie Bell, Freddie Miller, Eddie Shea, Davey Day, Jackie Sharkey, Pablo Dano, Albert "Chalky" Wright and Joey Silva. On August 30, 1934, he defeated Mike Belloise in fifteen rounds in New York to win the Featherweight Championship of the World (as recognized by New York state). He defeated Henry Armstrong twice although Armstrong afterwards defeated him three times, including the January 10, 1939 bout at the Olympic Auditorium, shown here, for the Welterweight Championship of the World. Arizmendi was elected to the International Boxing Hall of Fame in 2004.

A GOOD FIGHTER WITH A GOOD NAME. "Young" Peter Jackson tore through the rings of Los Angeles and the West Coast from 1930 to 1939. In that time, he won the Lightweight Championships of California and the Pacific Coast. He also won the Welterweight Championship of California. During his career, Jackson garnered wins over Ad Cadena, William "Goldie" Hess, Kenny LaSalle, Bobby Pacho, Don Fraser, Ah Wing Lee, Billy Townsend, Lew Massey, Battling Shaw, Ceferino Garcia, Tony Herrera, Cecil Payne, Sammy Fuller, Glen Lee, Johnny Datto, Frankie Klick, Joe "Young" Pimenthal and Frankie Britt.

QUICK FINISH. In his fourth professional bout, on November 13, 1934 at the Olympic Auditorium, Jacob "Buddy" Baer finished Gene Garner (going down) in 1:31 of the first round. Baer went on to be a top heavyweight contender and met Joe Louis in heavyweight title fights in 1941 and 1942. In the 1941 bout, Louis won by disqualification after the rowdy Baer resorted to rough tactics and actually put the champion out of the ring. Louis won the 1942 fight by a first round knockout. "Buddy" was a brother of Max Baer, the former Champion.

SLAPSIE MAXIE. Maxie Rosenbloom fought his first fight in the Los Angeles area in 1931. Afterwards, he fought here so often that he could have called it home. Fans were treated to the best fighters in the world as many of them came to town to fight Maxie. In all, Maxie fought here 31 times. Most of the time he won. But, on occasion, he lost. After all, he was in there with the best opposition and on a number of occasions, they were heavyweights. **(Courtesy J.J. Johnston)**

OSCAR. Oscar Rankin, who boxed from 1929-1941, was at the top of his game during 1933 through 1935 and appeared often in the area. The crafty "O" defeated such men as Bert Colima, William "Gorilla" Jones, Swede Berglund, Tait Littman, Solly Krieger, Young Terry, Al Quaill, Tommy Freeman, Sandy Garrison Casanova and Marty Simmons during his ring tenure.

ALWAYS A THREAT. Pablo Dano, a tough Filipino fighter, was a world class flyweight and bantamweight who had several long stints in California over a span from 1927-1938. Despite losing a number of bouts, it was a rare occasion that he was defeated in a decisive manner even when facing top fighters. Dano was managed by Jimmy Murray and Paddy Ryan at various times. **(Courtesy Antiquities of the Prize Ring)**

LIGHT-HEAVYWEIGHT CHAMP. John Henry Lewis was born in Los Angeles and boxed for nine years, from 1931 to 1939. During this time, he won more than 90 bouts, defeated some outstanding men and captured the Light Heavyweight Championship of the World in 1935. He also fought Joe Louis for the Heavyweight Championship in 1939. However, Lewis appeared in Los Angeles <u>only once</u>. On October 31, 1933, he defeated Frank Rowsey in ten rounds at the Olympic Auditorium in an unpopular decision.

DO IT THIS WAY, LITTLE MAN. Former heavyweight champion, Jack Johnson, on the left, explains technique to Young Tommy (Fernando Opao), an outstanding bantamweight battler of the early 1930s. Tommy won the Bantamweight Championship of the Orient in 1931 and the Bantamweight Championship of California in 1932. He lost the California Bantamweight title to Speedy Dado in 1932, won it back in 1933 and lost it again to Speedy that same year. **(Courtesy Antiquities of the Prize Ring)**

ANOTHER GOOD ONE. Joe Tei Ken (Jung Kwon Suh) was a terrific bantamweight of the early 1930s. Tei Ken began fighting in 1931 and had 32 bouts before he tasted his first defeat – against Young Tommy. He fought in the Los Angeles area on numerous occasions and during his career gained wins over such men as Yasu Hara, Eugene Huat, Hubert "Baby" Palmore, Little Pancho, Lew Farber, Small Montana, "Babe" Triscaro, Speedy Dado, Augie Curtis and Eddie Ceresoli.

Sports World Mourns "Uncle Tom's" Passing

Father of Local Boxing, He Brought Ring Stars to Los Angeles for Many Championship Bouts

BY DON ASHBAUGH

Uncle Tom is gone.

UNCLE TOM DEPARTS. Tom McCarey passed away on January 31, 1936 at St. Vincent's Hospital. The cause of death was heart ailment. He was 64 years of age. He had been associated with boxing for nearly fifty years.

SHOWED EARLY PROMISE. Three good, young California fighters in the early 1930s were Al Manfredo (left), Sammy O'Dell (center) and Frankie Castillo (right). Manfredo boxed out of Fresno, O'Dell fought mostly in Ohio and San Diego and Castillo made Hollywood his home. By 1937, Manfredo had beaten Ceferino Garcia two out of three bouts and had gone ten rounds with Fritzie Zivic and Glen Lee in losses. He experienced tough years in 1937 and 1938 that included losses to Barney Ross, Leon Zorrita and Eddie Booker. Knockout losses to Henry Armstrong in 1938 and 1939 brought an end to his career shortly afterwards. Major victories in Al's career came against Sammy Mandell, Eddie Ran, "Baby" Sal Sorio, Frankie Britt and Henry Schaft. Up to November, 1935, Castillo had a nice record that included wins over Speedy Dado and Young Tommy. O'Dell's best career wins came against "Indian" Mike Payan, Freddie Fitzgerald, Jackie Davis, Lloyd Smith, Billy Azevedo and Tony Roccaforte. Both O'Dell and Castillo had little success after 1935.

A WILLING TIGER. Glen Lee was born in Edison, Nebraska but made headlines in California during the mid-1930s. Reportedly, Lee won over forty amateur fights in 1932 and began fighting as a pro in the Midwest in 1933. In 1935, he came to California and boxed mostly in Los Angeles and Hollywood for the rest of his career. Lee gained victories over such men as Leon Zorrita, Bobby Pacho, Bep Van Klaveren, Ceferino Garcia, Izzy Jannazzo, Jackie Burke, Al Manfredo and Salvy Saban. Lee ventured to New York in 1937-1938 and battled against top flight competition. During his career, he fought some outstanding bouts against Fred Apostoli and Ceferino Garcia.

THE DEACON. Leo Kelly had a short career during the 1930s but a good one. The "Deacon" fought out of Los Angeles. During 1935-1937, he ventured to Australia and was highly successful. He defeated such men as Al Stillman, Tommy King, Ambrose Palmer, Ron Richards and Pietro Georgi during his time in the ring. **(Courtesy Antiquities of the Prize Ring)**

LEON ZORRITA. A top area fighter, Zorrita built up a fine record over the first three years of his career, 1933-1935, with only a draw and a single loss in nearly 30 bouts. He had a tougher time of it when he stepped up in competition but held his own. During his career, he gained wins over such men as Frankie Aragon, "Baby" Sal Sorio, Kenny LaSalle, Al Manfredo, Joe Bernal, Leonard Bennett, Kid Azteca, Bobby Pacho, Carmen Barth, Jimmy McDaniels and Vincente Villavicencio.

GONNA GITCHA. Lee Ramage (right) is shown tossing a right at King Levinsky in their April 7, 1936 bout at the Olympic Auditorium. This bout ended in a draw after ten rounds. In a three bout series in Los Angeles between the two, Levinsky won a ten-rounder on April 17, 1934 and Ramage won on July 7, 1936. The draw was sandwiched between these two encounters. Ramage was a world-class fighter - a good boxer with a nice punch. He fought mostly in San Diego and Los Angeles during the thirties.

HENRY, THE GREAT. Henry Armstrong defeated Alberto "Baby" Arizmendi in ten rounds on August 4, 1936 at Wrigley Field for the Featherweight Championship of the World (as recognized by both California and Mexico). On October 27 of the same year, at the Olympic Auditorium, Armstrong defeated Mike Belloise in ten rounds for his Featherweight title. Armstrong was back at the Olympic on January 10, 1939 for the Welterweight title bout in which he defeated Arizmendi and then, on October 24, a little more than nine months later, Henry defeated Jimmy Garrison in ten rounds at the Olympic to retain the Welterweight crown.

THE SWEDE. Milford "Swede" Berglund fought in the area for much of his career. Berglund had a fine record in the ring and defeated some outstanding men such as Johnny Adams, Al Trulmans, Joe Glick, Vearl Whitehead, Eddie Ran, Eddie "Babe" Risko, Solly Krieger, Andy Divodi, Ben Jeby, Johnny "Bandit" Romero, Ray Actis, Paul Pirrone and Young Stuhley.

CARLOS. Carlos Miranda (on the left), shown here with Chris Cardenas, had a long career with most bouts taking place in the 1930s. He had an up-and-down career and was at his best during 1936-1937. Miranda had wins over Angus "Angie" Smith, Georgie Crouch, Charley Bedami, Jimmy Brooks and Joe Gavras and draws with Louie Flyer and Black Bill (Humberto Rejon). He also fought some tough fights against Henry Woods, Jimmy Garrison, Jimmy McDaniels and Leon Zorrita.

CRAFTY JACK. In 1936, his first year in the ring, Jack Chase lost but a single bout in 19 contests. His next best year was 1942 when he lost once in 17 bouts. Chase was the Welterweight Champion of Colorado and the Middleweight and Light Heavyweight Champion of California during his career. He beat such men as Archie Moore, Eddie Booker, Harry "Kid" Matthews, Lloyd Marshall, Leon Zorrita, "Oakland" Billy Smith, Aaron Wade, Eddie Murdock, Reuben Shank, Willard "Big Boy" Hogue, Jimmy McDaniels, Watson Jones and Kenny Watkins. Quite a record !

HANDLED MEN, HANDLED EVENTS. Stephen "Suey" Welch took over as matchmaker at the Olympic Auditorium for a short time during 1937. His first big fight was the March 23 contest between Alberto "Baby" Arizmendi and Wally Hally. "Suey" made his name as the manager of good fighters – William "Gorilla" Jones, Ellsworth "Hank" Hankinson, Charley Powell and "Irish" Gil King - to name four. Welch was also a good friend of George Parnassus.

A FINE FIGHTER. Kenny LaSalle fought more than 100 bouts between 1929-1948. He was at his best during 1929-1932 and 1937-1938. During his career, he earned wins over many "name" fighters including Fritzie Zivic, Benny Garcia, Johnny Lamar, Tod Morgan, Battling Dozier, Steve Halaiko, Tracy Cox, Izzy Jannazzo, Andre Jesserun, George Salvadore, Kid Azteca, "Young" Peter Jackson, "Wild" Bill McDowell, Carl Dell and Paulie Peters.

THE OLYMPIC. Here is a view of the Olympic Auditorium in 1938. It was the site of many famous bouts over the years including a large number of title contests. After 80 years of boxing and other entertainment, the Olympic was sold in August, 2005, to a Korean church group. **(Courtesy SECURITY PACIFIC COLLECTION / Los Angeles Public Library)**

TOUGH COMPETITOR. Tony Chavez boxed frequently in Los Angeles and Hollywood from 1932-1946. During this time he defeated many good men including Henry Armstrong, Gene Espinosa, Ritchie Fontaine, Pete DeGrasse, Frankie Terranova, Abie Israel, Hubert "Kid" Dennis, Jimmy Garrison, Georgie Crouch, Georgie Hansford and Mike Belloise. **(Courtesy Antiquities of the Prize Ring)**

DOWN YOU GO. Gunnar Barlund is shown flooring Chuck Crowell in the April 19, 1938 bout at the Olympic Auditorium on his way to a ten round decision. Barlund was a top heavyweight from Europe who invaded the United States in 1936 and built up an impressive record. Crowell was a California man who stood 6-5 and weighed 220 pounds. He fought from 1937-1946 and was a good boxer who sported more than 20 wins with 14 knockouts going into this bout with Barlund. During his career, Crowell earned wins over Nash Garrison, Tony Souza, George "Sonny Boy" Walker, Sandy McDonald, Bob Nestell, Johnny Erjavac, Ellsworth "Hank" Hankinson, Ford Smith, Al Delaney and Charley Belanger.

GARCIA WHIPS GLEN LEE AT GILMORE STADIUM

Filipino Scores Surprising Upset to Give Nebraska Wildcat Sound Drubbing

Ceferino Garcia spotted Glen Lee nearly ten pounds in weight and a 10-8 bulge in the betting odds but came through with a decisive ten-round victory over the Nebraskan in the Hollywood Legion's summer opener at Gilmore Stadium last night.

GARCIA TAKES LEE. On May 6, 1938 at Gilmore Stadium, Ceferino Garcia defeated Glen Lee in ten rounds before about 10,000 fans. Garcia won the fight on rounds 6-3-1 in spite of the fact that he was outweighed 154 pounds to 145 ½. Abe Roth was the referee.

A TALENTED YOUNG MAN. Ritchie Fontaine was a native of Montana as was one of the authors of this book, Chuck Johnston. Ritchie began his career in the Montana and Washington area but became an attraction in the Los Angeles area in the mid 1930s. Ritchie owned wins over such men as Henry Armstrong, future featherweight champion Jackie Wilson, Jimmy Thomas, Pete DeGrasse, Tony Chavez and Everett "Young" Rightmire. He also had draw verdicts against Holman Williams, Hubert "Kid" Dennis, Nick Peters and Georgie Hansford. **(Courtesy J.J. Johnston)**

FLY BOY. "Lefty" Louie Flyer (on the left) had a fine record over an eleven year career and was at his best during 1936-1938 although 1946 was a good year. In his time, Flyer had victories over such men as Bobby Pacho and Lew Jenkins and draws against Henry Woods, Jimmy McDaniels and Sixto Morales.

HEY THERE, GEORGIE BOY. Georgie Hansford had a long and successful career, fighting from 1930-1947 and winning nearly 100 contests. His best performance year was 1932 when he had more than 20 bouts and lost just one. During his career, Hansford defeated such men as Joe "Young" Pimenthal, Benny Garcia, Andy Bundy, Gregorio Vidal, Johnny Pena, Tommy Paul, Gene Espinosa, Varias Milling, Pete DeGrasse, Everett "Young" Rightmire, Nick Peters, Tony Chavez and Freddie Miller. **(Courtesy J.J. Johnston)**

CAPACITY CROWD TURNS OUT FOR GALA OPENING OF NEW $250,000 HOLLYWOOD LEGION ARENA

NEW FACILITY. On September 2, 1938, some 6,000 fans turned out to see the new Hollywood Legion Arena. Georgie Hansford and Quentin "Baby" Breese fought a savage, vicious exchange of leather in the main attraction to a ten round draw. In the semi-final bout, scrappy Frank Rowsey, another area fighter, defeated Paul Hartnek in six rounds.

GOOD NIGHT, SWEET PRINCE. Lou Nova (back to camera) was a world-class heavyweight who was born in Los Angeles but engaged in only six bouts in the area during his career. A rough and ready fighter from the go, Nova tangled with 6'4" Phil Brubaker (shown down) in Oakland on September 7, 1938. Going into the fight, Lou had only one loss in more than twenty bouts, with ten knockouts to his credit. Brubaker's record was six losses in 37 contests, with 1 "No Decision" and 17 knockouts. Nova won this bout in one round. Nine months later, Lou knocked out former heavyweight champion, Max Baer, and then lost to Tony Galento in Philadelphia in one of the dirtiest fights in boxing annals.

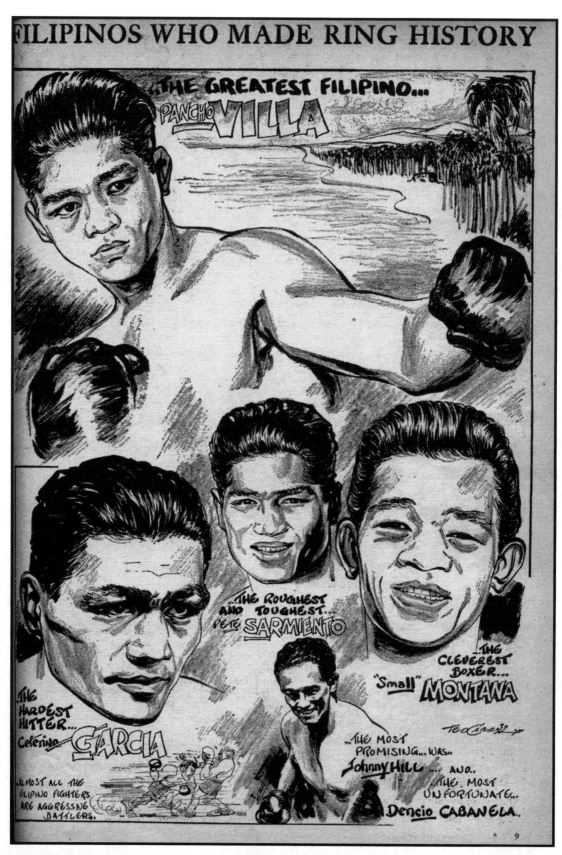

OUTSTANDING FILIPINO FIGHTERS. Some of the great Filipino fighters are credited here. Pancho Villa is called the greatest of the group while Ceferino Garcia is labeled as the hardest hitter and Pete Sarmiento is pegged as the roughest and toughest. Small Montana is called the cleverest, Johnny Hill the most promising and Dencio Cabanela the most unfortunate. Only Villa did not fight in the area.

WELL-RESPECTED. Bob Nestell began fighting professionally in 1936 and was an outstanding heavyweight prospect by mid-1937. Nestell had been a successful amateur who posted a 28-1 record. He was a clever boxer and hard hitter who impressed many who saw him in action. Among the sportswriters who held him in high regard as one of the best looking young boxers in years were Jack Singer, Sid Ziff, Gene Coughlin, Bill Potts, Bob Hebert, Bob Cronin, Braven Dyer and Bob Ray. Boxing people such as Al Lang, Eddie Mead, "Suey" Welch, George Parnassus, Joe Waterman, Tom Gallery, Jerry Pelton, Tony Palazolo, Johnny Keyes, "Babe" McCoy, Bill Miller, Mushy Greenston and Claude Greenston praised his skills too. Among those he defeated during his career were King Levinsky, Lee Ramage, George "Sonny Boy" Walker, Frank Rowsey, Nash Garrison, Chuck Crowell and Sandy McDonald.

BIG AL. Alphonse "Big Boy" Bray was big and strong at 6-4 and fighting between 204 and 218 pounds. He fought during 1936-1941 and won the Heavyweight Championship of California during his career. He beat such men as Lee Savold, Ellsworth "Hank" Hankinson, Jack Roper, Sal Ruggirello, Eddie Simms, Abe Simon, Chuck Crowell and Yancey Henry.

SCRAPPY GEORGIE. Georgie Crouch fought mostly in Los Angeles during his short career that lasted from 1935-1941. During this time, he defeated such men as Nick Peters, Jimmy Garrison, Ritchie Fontaine, Tony Chavez, Phil Zwick, Johnny Fasano, Clever Henry and Johnny Dias. **(Courtesy J.J. Johnston)**

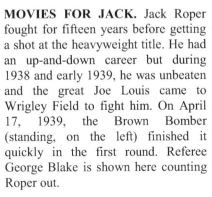

MOVIES FOR JACK. Jack Roper fought for fifteen years before getting a shot at the heavyweight title. He had an up-and-down career but during 1938 and early 1939, he was unbeaten and the great Joe Louis came to Wrigley Field to fight him. On April 17, 1939, the Brown Bomber (standing, on the left) finished it quickly in the first round. Referee George Blake is shown here counting Roper out.

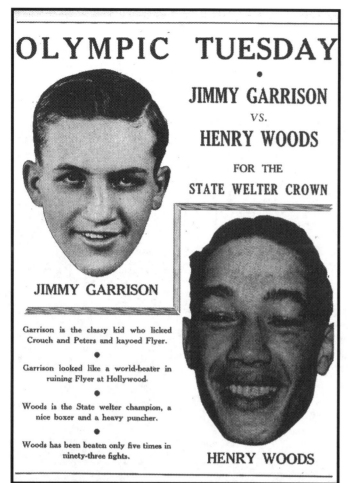

OLYMPIC TUESDAY

JIMMY GARRISON
VS.
HENRY WOODS

FOR THE
STATE WELTER CROWN

JIMMY GARRISON

Garrison is the classy kid who licked
Crouch and Peters and kayoed Flyer.

Garrison looked like a world-beater in
ruining Flyer at Hollywood.

Woods is the State welter champion, a
nice boxer and a heavy puncher.

Woods has been beaten only five times in
ninety-three fights.

HENRY WOODS

GARRISON-WOODS. Henry Woods and Jimmy Garrison were two fine fighters with excellent records. They tangled twice in Los Angeles in 1939. Woods took the first encounter in a ten round decision on May 23. Almost exactly six months later, Garrison won their second battle with a fifth round technical knockout. Many observers thought this bout was perhaps fixed because Garrison was already scheduled to fight Henry Armstrong for the World Welterweight title. **(Courtesy J.J. Johnston)**

Negro Boxers Appear at Hollywood Legion

Richard Polite Tangles With Lemos in First
Bout Under Film Stadium's New Ring Policy

BLACK BOXERS CAN APPEAR. On January 20, 1940, the State Athletic Commission of California persuaded officials at the Hollywood Legion Stadium to permit Negro boxers to appear on boxing cards held there.

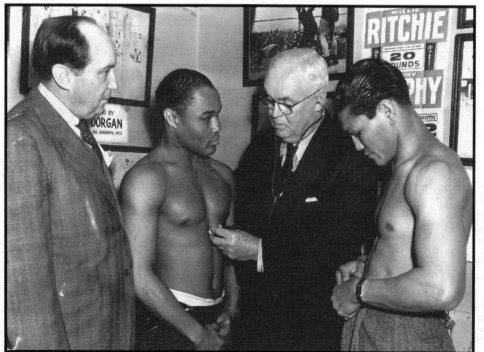

CHECKING OUT THE BOYS. California's State Athletic Commission ordered Henry Armstrong to go through with his contracted fight of March 1, 1940 at Gilmore Stadium with Ceferino Garcia or be suspended. Armstrong, Welterweight Champion, and Ceferino Garcia, Middleweght Champion, are shown taking the official physicals by the State Athletic Commission prior to their fight for Garcia's crown. Left to right, are Jerry Giesler, Commission chairman, Armstrong, Dr. Lloyd R. Mace and Garcia. Geisler was a famous attorney who represented celebrities. The Middleweight Championship fight ended in a ten round draw. **(Courtesy HERALD-EXAMINER COLLECTION / Los Angeles Public Library)**

HOLLYWOOD GETS INTO THE ACT. *Ex-Champ*, a Universal-International Motion Picture Production of 1939, featured Victor McLaglen, Tom Brown, William Frawley, Noble "Kid" Chissell, Marc Lawrence and Sam Hinds. In this scene, McLaglen (left, in the boxing pose), who once boxed a six-round bout with former Heavyweight Champion, Jack Johnson, engaged in a sparring session with Chissell, a former United States Navy Middleweight Champion.

GOOD FIGHTER, GOOD REFEREE. George Latka (on the left) was a very good lightweight during 1937-1942 who gained victories over Georgie Hansford, Georgie Crouch, Alberto "Baby" Arizmendi, Quentin "Baby" Breese, Jimmy Garrison, Nick Peters, Petey Scalzo and Ritchie Lemos. After he retired from boxing, George became a famous referee and handled ten world title bouts in the Los Angeles area during 1961-1975. Here, he is seen with famous movie actor, George Raft. **(Courtesy J.J. Johnston)**

A VERY GOOD WELTERWEIGHT. Eddie Marcus began his career in 1938 and kept punching until 1947. During this time, he fought a draw with Alberto "Baby" Arizmendi, a three bout series with Richie Lemos, in which they each won once (the other verdict being a draw), gained wins over Al Lust, Eddie Hudson, Vic Grupico, Laurie Peterson, Sel Hamilton and earned a draw against Jimmy Doyle.

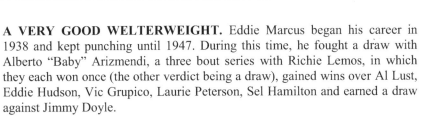

GREAT FIGHTS, GREAT TIMES. Fans were getting such good shows at the Olympic Boxing Club, they were eager for the next fight card to come about. Joe Lynch was the promoter and matchmaker for the club located at 1801 South Grand Avenue in Los Angeles.

FIGHTS AT JEFFRIES BARN. Here is a copy of the *Barn News*, a publication for the Jeffries Barn fight card on July 18, 1940. It contains an article about Jimmy Martin and lists the fights for the evening. For this card, nine bouts were scheduled - Frank Flores vs. Mario Luna, Bob Grinkie vs. Andy Medina, Frank Russell vs. Al Filda, Bob Stringer vs. Nils Anderson, Mike Repovitch vs. Mike DeLaRosa, Ray Miller vs. Russ Metcalf, Blackie Stevens vs. Mel Smith and Ray Vargas vs. Dandy Davis. The main event was between Jimmy Martin and Jim Wilson. The Barn was an outstanding location for amateur bouts during its lifetime. Jim Jeffries was owner and manager.

JAS. J. JEFFRIES Owner and Mgr. ED. J. FARRELL Matchmaker JOS. P. EGAN Exec. Box Office For Reservations Call CHarleston 6-1169	**The** **BARN NEWS** A publication devoted to the interests of Amateur Boxing SUGGESTING THE BEST PRESENTING THE BEST — PRICES — Ringside—Two Rows _____ $1.10 Reserved—Canvas Chairs _____ .85 Individual Wood Chairs _____ .55 Bleacher Admission _____ .35	GEO. O'BRIEN Superintendent Marie Middlekauf Cashier Irene O'Brien Asst. Cashier Helen Scheuer, Press Rep.

Vol. No. 7   Thursday, July 18, 1940   No. 28

JAMES J. JEFFRIES

Presents

FRANK FLORES Los Angeles	vs. 119	MARIO LUNA Los Angeles
BOB GRINKIE Hollywood	vs. 132	ANDY MEDINA Los Angeles

TICKET BOOST DUE TO NEW TAX
Commencing tonight, the 35 cent seats at Jeffries Barn will be advanced to 40 cents. The price boost will cover the newly imposed Federal Defense tax which has been ordered this month by the government on all amusement and sports tickets, which previously hadn't been subject to a government tax.

WHAT TO EXPECT
What Tony Canelli is to Lincoln Heights, Jimmy Martin is to Glendale—which means that a big delegation of Glendale folk will be on hand at the Barn tonight to support Jimmy when he starts his long awaited comeback.
Martin, the hero of many a terrific bout at the Barn during the last two years, has been out of the ring for several months, due to a painful nose operation. But now, after his convalescence in the mountains, he's as fit as the proverbial

Jimmy Martin

fiddle, and rarin' to go, according to his trainer and ardent supporter, Manny Vasquez.
The Glendale boy, who by the

TALENTED MAN PASSES. Hayden "Wad" Wadhams died on April 17, 1941 in Rancho Los Amigos, following a long illness. He was a pioneer in California fistic circles and was one of Southern California's most widely known boxing figures. Wadhams was famous as a matchmaker of championship matches.

SNOWY. Reginald "Snowy" Baker had a short tenure in the early 1940s as the promoter at the Olympic Auditorium. "Snowy" lived a colorful life. He was one of the greatest all-around athletes in his native Australia and won a silver medal while boxing as a middleweight in the 1908 Olympics. After a stint of a few years as the premier Australian boxing promoter, Baker became a pioneer silent movie star in his native country. While residing in the Los Angeles area, starting in the 1920s, Baker was well-known as a polo player and the longtime head of Los Angeles Athletic Club's Riviera Polo Grounds.

TITLE CHANGED HANDS. On July 1, 1941, Richie Lemos (left) knocked out Petey Scalzo in five rounds at the Olympic Auditorium to win the NBA Featherweight Championship. Scalzo fought out of New York and had been declared Featherweight Champion by the NBA on May 1, 1940. He had retained his title in defenses against Frankie Covelli, Bobby "Poison" Ivy and Phil Zwick. Scalzo had knocked out Richie in a previous match on December 27, 1940 in Hollywood and boasted a record of 80 wins, 5 losses and 6 draws when he met Lemos for the title. Lemos, out of Los Angeles, had a good record but not sterling with 38 wins, 10 losses and 2 draws in 50 contests at the time the title match was held. After winning the title from Scalzo, he lost the crown in his first defense. Richie passed away in October of 2004. **(Courtesy J.J. Johnston)**

OUTSTANDING MAN. Charles Eyton, motion picture pioneer during the silent film era and boxing referee, died on July 2, 1941 at the Hollywood Hospital. He was Production and General Manager of the old Famous Players-Lasky Corporation and then General Manager of the Paramount Studios. He married actress Kathlyn Williams, star of silent films, in 1916. They divorced in 1931 but remained true friends. During his career as a boxing referee, he was the main referee at Hazard's Pavilion and "Uncle" Tom McCarey's promotions at the Naud Junction Pavilion and Vernon Arena. He officiated 23 major world championship bouts and even more if the "Colored" championships are included.

PASSES — Charles F. Eyton, pioneer film man.

Eyton, Screen Pioneer, Dies

Kathlyn Williams of Silent Era, His Divorced Wife, With Him at End

Hollywood lost another motion-picture pioneer yesterday when Charles F. Eyton, executive in the silent era of the industry and former husband of Kathlyn Williams, star of silent films, died at Hollywood Hospital. He was 70 and his death was attributed to pneumonia which he contracted five days ago.

The sporting world will also mourn Eyton's passing for he was once considered the greatest prize fight referee of his time.

SECOND CHAMP FROM L.A. Here, Albert "Chalky" Wright (left) spars with "Young" Peter Jackson. Wright won a version of the Featherweight Championship of the World on September 11, 1941 when he defeated Joey Archibald. The Featherweight division had two world champions at this time (Wright and Richie Lemos) and both men fought often in the *City of Angels*. "Chalky" held the title for a little over a year and then lost it to Willie Pep. During his great career, Wright fought from 1928 to 1948 and engaged in more than 200 bouts. He was elected to the International Boxing Hall of Fame in 1997. **(Courtesy Antiquities of the Prize Ring)**

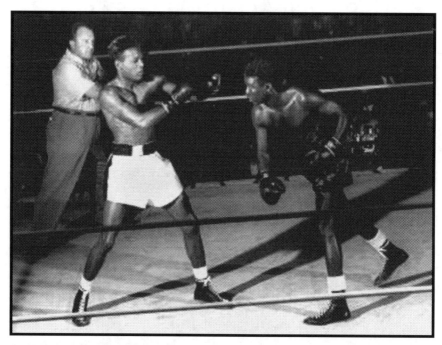

SIZZLER. Here, late in his career, "California" Jackie Wilson (right) misses a right swing at "Sugar" Ray Robinson at the Olympic on October 28, 1947. Robinson won by a seventh round stoppage. Wilson, from Los Angeles, fought from the mid-1930s through 1949 and during this time won the Welterweight Championship of California. From late 1938 through early 1943, he fought 38 bouts and lost only one. During his career, he won over such men as Henry Woods, Jackie Burke, John Thomas, Ritchie Fontaine, Eddie Cool, Tony Chavez, Jimmy Garrison, Georgie Crouch, Alberto "Baby" Arizmendi, Larry Cisneros, Kid Azteca, Ceferino Garcia, Cocoa Kid, Fritzie Zivic, "Young" Peter Jackson and Tommy Bell.

Chapter Five

The Babe McCoy Era

1942-1956

With the entrance of the United States into World War II, the **Great Depression** truly ended and many changes took place in the Los Angeles area. Manufacturing increased dramatically to meet the tremendous demands of waging the biggest war in history. The most obvious growth took place in the production of airplanes.

As a result of the huge manufacturing surge, the number of working people, including women, increased. There were many military installations in California (and Los Angeles). War materials and servicemen were shipped to the war fronts from all major ports in the state. Many of these workers and servicemen were boxing fans and - they had money to spend.

In the Southwest, a large number of American-born children of Mexican immigrants (who came to the United States in huge numbers starting in 1917) became adults by the beginning of World War II. Many other Mexicans came to the United States for the first time since the beginning of the **Great Depression** because of the strong demand for workers. Subsequently, the boxing crowds included more and more fans of Mexican descent and they became the major fan base in Los Angeles boxing during the latter part of the Twentieth Century.

During 1942, a colorful Australian named Reginald "Snowy" Baker became involved in promoting boxing cards at the Olympic Auditorium. In an interesting life, Baker was a top all-around athlete, a major boxing promoter and a pioneer star in action movies before migrating to the United States during the early 1920s. Here, he continued his movie career with varying success in Hollywood. While living in the Los Angeles area, Baker became involved with the LAAC and was hired by Frank Garbutt to do a number of jobs, notably develop and manage the LAAC's Riviera Polo Fields.

Under Baker, Joe Waterman worked as the matchmaker at the Olympic Auditorium, until he left the post due to ill health. His successor was his protégé, "Babe" McCoy (Harry Rudolph McCoy), the brother of Al McCoy, the former World Middleweight champion and manager of boxers. In addition to working his new job at the Olympic Auditorium, McCoy also continued, for a short time, as matchmaker at the thriving small boxing club in Ocean Park.

A number of old-timers remember McCoy as the driving force at the Olympic Auditorium from 1942 to 1956. With "Babe" as the matchmaker, there were many boxing cards staged at the Olympic Auditorium and at Wrigley Field with quite a bit of success.

In 1943, Baker made way for Cal Eaton, a state boxing inspector, and Aileen Lebell (later, Aileen Eaton), who worked for the LAAC and Frank Garbutt. Eaton functioned as promoter while Lebell acted as business manager. Under the new management, McCoy continued as the matchmaker.

During the 1940s, other venues staged professional boxing cards in the Los Angeles area besides the Olympic Auditorium, the Hollywood Legion Stadium and the Ocean Park Arena. Joe Lynch, the one-time promoter at the Olympic Auditorium, staged some large boxing shows at Gilmore Field (the home of the Pacific Coast League Baseball Club, the Hollywood Stars) during World War II. Other local venues included the Wilmington Bowl and South Gate.

A Mexican-American boxer from El Centro, the great Manuel Ortiz, was in his heyday during the 1940s. As the World Bantamweight Champion during a period spanning from 1942 to 1950, he was an excellent drawing card. One of the greatest fighters of Mexican descent ever, he was also regarded as one of the best bantamweights in history.

The most popular boxer in Los Angeles during the 1940s was another Mexican-American, a lightweight named Enrique Bolanos. He drew huge crowds at both the Olympic Auditorium and Wrigley Field on a frequent basis - the largest gates in Los Angeles since Ace Hudkins' big crowds during the late 1920s. In his career, Bolanos got three chances at the World Lightweight Title held by Ike Williams, all at Wrigley Field. Other popular Los Angeles-based fighters who were active during the 1940s included Fabela Chavez, Carlos Chavez, John Thomas, Jimmy Doyle and Hilton "Fitzie" Fitzpatrick.

During the middle 1940s, a young fighter from New Mexico named Art Aragon became one of the most colorful boxers in Los Angeles boxing history. He was a top fighter in both the lightweight and welterweight divisions and the biggest, most consistent drawing card in Los Angeles during the 1950s.

In late 1947, the highly successful matchmaker at the Hollywood Legion Stadium, Charley MacDonald, resigned after sixteen years on the job. During the remaining twelve years of its existence, the Hollywood Legion Stadium experienced a mixture of successes and setbacks. Bobby Jackson was a temporary matchmaker from January 1, 1948 to July 2, 1948.

Boxing benefited from a tremendous boom in sports in the United States (and other parts of the world) during the late 1940s. There were many boxing clubs that drew huge crowds. Other professional sports that attracted huge crowds during this period included baseball (both major league and minor league) and automobile racing.

However, this sports boom in the United States proved to be short-lived, largely due to the advent of television during the late 1940s and early 1950s. More and more people stayed home to watch television and attendance suffered at many sporting events, including boxing shows.

Many minor league baseball teams (as well as minor leagues themselves), auto racing venues and boxing clubs went out of business by the end of the 1950s. Few boxing venues emerged unscathed. At the same time, boxing became a popular staple of television programming and many fighters became famous across the entire nation.

Over the years, as a result of the boxing shows on television, many fans remembered the 1950s fondly. However, by the end of the 1950s, a number of longtime boxing venues in the area ceased to exist, including the Wilmington Bowl, Ocean Park Arena and Hollywood Legion Stadium. Still, the area continued to be a relative hotbed of boxing activity, even to the present time.

On July 2, 1948, Baron Henry Von Stumme, the colorful former manager of Chuck Crowell and Richie Lemos, became the matchmaker at the Hollywood Legion Stadium. Von Stumme's two-year stint was a stormy one. During his first year, he got into quarrels with a group of boxing managers about the purses for boxers. In the first months of 1950, attendance dropped and many felt that poor matches were the cause. However, Von Stumme contended that the culprit was television. Consequently, he handed in his resignation on May 15, 1950, effective on June 2, 1950.

Another veteran manager, Cal Working, became the matchmaker at the Legion Stadium on June 9, 1950. Working was credited with increasing the attendance by staging good bouts. Even mediocre main events were drawing crowds numbering 2,500 just a few weeks before Working's resignation in October, 1953.

After serving as an aide under Von Stumme and as assistant matchmaker under Working, Gabriel "Hap" Navarro became matchmaker at the Hollywood Legion Stadium on October 1, 1953. While with Working, Navarro put together most of the preliminary matches. During his two-year stint, Navarro staged a number of bouts drawing record-breaking gates before resigning on October 1, 1955.

Jackie Leonard, a noted boxing manager and the assistant matchmaker under Navarro, then became the matchmaker at the Hollywood Legion Stadium. During a very unstable period, there were numerous headline-making stories involving Leonard and the Hollywood Legion Stadium over the next four years.

Art Aragon was the top drawing card in the area during the 1950s but there were other Los Angeles-based boxers who were popular too. They included Don Jordan (who went on to become a World Welterweight Champion), Gil Cadilli, Ignacio "Keeny" Teran, Clarence Henry, Willie Vaughn, Charley Green, Cisco Andrade and Billy Peacock.

A state investigation into corruption in boxing during the middle 1950s resulted in the powerful matchmaker of the Olympic Auditorium, "Babe" McCoy, being banned for life due to charges that he was an "underground" manager of boxers and that he fixed a number of bouts.

AN OUTSTANDING FIGHTER AND CHAMPION. Born in Corona, California, Manuel Ortiz began fighting in 1938 in Hollywood and Los Angeles and fought here often throughout his career. Following an up-and-down start, he posted a 4-1-1 mark in 1940 followed by an 8-1-1 record in 1941. From 1942 on, he was truly a world class fighter and someone to be reckoned with until 1949. From late 1941 to late 1946, he lost only to Willie Pep. On August 7, 1942, Ortiz won the Bantamweight Championship of the World by defeating Lou Salica in twelve rounds at the Legion Stadium in Hollywood. In 1943, he defended his crown eight times, including defenses in Long Beach, Hollywood and Los Angeles. He successfully retained his title four times in Los Angeles during 1944. Ortiz had three more winning defenses in 1946, with one of them held in Hollywood. Harold Dade defeated him on January 6, 1947 in San Francisco to take the crown but Ortiz won it back two months later at the Olympic Auditorium. After this, Manuel won title contests four more times and reigned as the Bantam king until May 31, 1950, when he lost his crown to Vic Toweel in fifteen rounds in Johannesburg, South Africa.

AN ALL-TIME GREAT. Here, "Hap" Navarro (on the left) awards Ortiz (right) with a trophy, in the 1950s, as one of the All-Time great boxers from the Los Angeles area. **(Courtesy Lupe Ortiz Saldana)**

HAIN'T NO TURKEY. Albert "Turkey" Thompson, with his trainer, wasn't a big heavyweight but he sure could fight. Fighting from 1938-1952, Albert tangled with the best in the world and held his own. He began his career as a middleweight and won 24 bouts during the first three years. In January of 1941, he won the Heavyweight Championship of California. His peak period was probably from August, 1941 to April, 1944, when he engaged in 18 fights and lost only one. During his career, he defeated such men as Bobby Pacho, Willard "Big Boy" Hogue, Glen Lee, Junior Munsell, Teddy Yarosz, Tommy Martin, Johnny "Bandit" Romero, Charles "Buddy" Knox, Pat Valentino, Gus Dorazio, Eddie Blunt, Elmer "Violent" Ray, Chuck Crowell, Johnny Haynes, Arturo Godoy, Tony Bosnich, Willie Bean and Lee Q. Murray. Yes sir, "Turkey" could take care of himself. **(Courtesy Antiquities of the Prize Ring)**

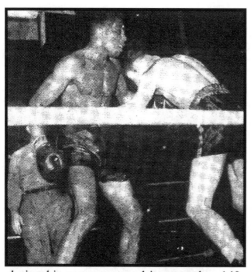

SAMMY BEATS THE SLUGGER. In this photo, on October 27, 1943, at Gilmore Field, Sammy Angott (on the right) defeats Luther "Slugger" White in fifteen rounds to win the NBA Lightweight Championship. Angott had retired on November 13, 1942 and relinquished his crown but, in January of 1943, he announced his return to the ring. Sammy was inducted into the International Boxing Hall of Fame in 1998.

CLEVER MEXICAN FIGHTER. Juan Zurita (Juan Bautista Zurita Ferrer) began fighting in Mexico in 1932 and during his career engaged in more than 140 contests, winning 121. Along the way, he was the Featherweight and Lightweight Champion of Mexico. On March 8, 1944, at the Hollywood Legion Stadium, Zurita defeated Sammy Angott in a fifteen rounder to capture the NBA Lightweight Championship of the World. A little over a year later, on April 18, 1945, he lost that title when he was stopped by Ike Williams in two rounds in Mexico City. **(Courtesy Antiquities of the Prize Ring)**

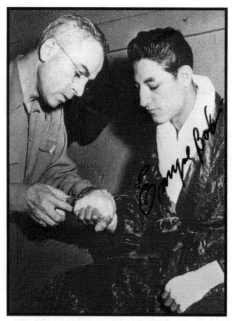

FIX 'EM UP GOOD, POPS. Enrique Bolanos gets his hands wrapped by his manager, George Parnassus, prior to a battle. Bolanos was a home-grown Los Angeles fighter of considerable talent. He began fighting in 1943 and by 1946 had compiled a record of 24-3 with his only losses going to Luis Castillo, Manuel Ortiz and Albert "Chalky" Wright. **(Courtesy Clay Moyle)**

WATSON JONES. Watson had a lengthy career, beginning in 1938. He was very good from January, 1940 to April, 1943, when he won 17 bouts. After this, until he retired in 1956, his career was up-and-down. In 1956, Jones testified at the "Babe" McCoy legal hearings that McCoy had fixed a number of fights in the Los Angeles area. **(Courtesy J.J. Johnston)**

GOLDEN GLOVES TOURNAMENT. Always an exciting time to see young, aspiring boxers go at it. Shown here is a program from the 1944 Boxing Tournament sponsored by the Los Angeles Times.

BATTLING BENNY. "Battling" Benny Goldberg is shown with his manager, Pete Reilly. He was an outstanding fighter and the Bantamweight Champion of Michigan at one time. Benny found a following in the Los Angeles area from the late 1930s to the mid 1940s. The battler lost only a couple of fights during his entire career and whipped such men as Luis Castillo, Tony Olivera, Joey Archibald, Manuel Ortiz, George Annarino, Jimmy Gilligan and Carlos "No No" Cuebas. Benny was inducted into the World Boxing Hall of Fame in 1994. **(Courtesy J.J. Johnston)**

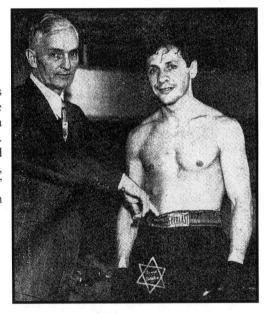

SLICK HAROLD. Here, Harold Dade (on the right) receives the Bantamweight title belt from Harry Winkler at the Olympic Auditorium. Dade fought often in the Los Angeles area, especially during his early career when he racked up a 19-1-2 record. In 1947, he defeated Manuel Ortiz for the World Bantamweight Championship and then lost it back to him two months afterwards in a bout at the Olympic Auditorium. Later that year, he fought a draw with Carlos Chavez for the Featherweight Championship of California. In 1948, Harold defeated Lauro Salas twice but from that time until he retired in 1955, won only a few bouts.

A WORLD CLASS FIGHTER. Carlos Chavez was a talented boxer who began boxing in Hollywood in 1939 and fought into the 1950s. From 1939-1944, he experienced only three losses, two of them to Manuel Ortiz. During this time, he won 25 bouts and defeated such men as Lou Salica, Tony Olivera and Al Medrano. From 1945-1949, he stepped up in competition and won 22 contests, including wins over Ortiz, Harold Dade, Lefty LaChance, Charley "Cabey" Lewis, Alfredo Escobar and Lauro Salas. He made progress up the Featherweight ladder under the careful management of Johnny Forbes, was the Featherweight Champion of California in 1947 and a top contender for the World title held by Willie Pep. At this time, several attempts had been made to get Pep and Phil Terranova in the ring with Chavez to no avail. His career began to slide in 1950 and he was defeated a number of times although he managed to defeat Art Aragon. Chavez fought through 1956. He was shot and killed in 1990. Carlos was inducted into the World Boxing Hall of Fame in 1991.

MR. TROUBLE. Kenny Watkins was a classy boxer who fought from the early 1940s until 1951. From 1942-1945, Watkins rang up 28 victories. During his career, he defeated such men as Jack Chase, Kenny LaSalle, George Evans, Milo Savage and "Irish" Bob Murphy.

L.A. BATTLER. Frankie Angustain was active in local rings from 1943-1950 and gained some nice victories over the likes of Earl Turner, Charley Cato, Mel Brown, Max Hutchins, Jackie Ryan and Andy Faison. In addition, he had draws against Jimmy Brooks and Roy Miller.

DO IT LIKE THIS, FELLOWS. Famous musician, Harry James (center), shows Jimmy Doyle (left) and Jimmy McDaniels how to toot the horn. Doyle, who boxed in the area during the early to mid-1940s, was an outstanding welterweight who had won 29 of 30 bouts just prior to his fatal fight with "Sugar" Ray Robinson in 1947. Jimmy died as the result of injuries sustained during the contest. McDaniels boxed from the late 1930s through early 1947. He was at his best from 1938-1940 when he won 20 bouts. But, from 1941 until the end of his career, times got tougher as he stepped up in competition. **(Courtesy "Hap" Navarro)**

BEWARE OF THE SPIDER. "Spider" Mock (Gene Jensen) assists Jimmy Florita to his feet after stopping him at the Coliseum in San Diego on January 4, 1946. Mock made a name for himself during his amateur career of nearly 200 bouts, many fought at Jeffries' Barn during the mid-late 1930s. Like a spider, he moved quickly and tied up his opponent for the kill. He carried a stinging right hand punch and a quick left hook. Mock had a short but decent professional career that was hindered by World War II. After the war, he boxed a little more but then went into motion picture acting.

BABE. Babe "Hardrock" Gordon (George Edwards) built a nice ring record for himself in area rings although he never reached the upper echelons of the heavyweight division. Starting in 1943, he did not lose until nearly three years later. During his career, he had wins against George "Baby Dutch" Culbertson, Joe Knight and Hank Thurman and fought draws with Freddie Beshore and George Parmentier.

ALFREDO AND FABELA. In a great five bout rivalry during 1946-1947, Alfredo Escobar defeated Fabela Chavez three times to two. Four of the bouts were held in either Los Angeles or Hollywood. Here, Escobar (left) lands on Chavez in their April 8, 1947 contest at the Olympic Auditorium. Alfredo captured a ten round decision in this one.

TWO GOOD 'UNS. Larry Cisneros (left) is shown with referee, Joe Louis, in 1947. Cisneros was a capable, scrappy fighter who first appeared in Hollywood in 1940. Larry was not a power hitter but had wonderful boxing savvy. He began fighting in 1937 and posted a 29-3 record through 1939. As he stepped up in competition, he compiled an 11-1-1 record in 1940 and 7-4-2 in 1941. Over the next five years, Cisneros won 20 bouts as his skills began to decline. During his career, he scored wins over such men as Johnny Hutchinson, Richard "Sheik" Rangel, Sammy Brown, Norman Rubio, Roman Alvarez, George "Sugar" Costner, Joey Varoff and Albert "Chalky" Wright.

TWO OUT OF THREE. On June 23, 1947, "Jersey" Joe Walcott (on the left) won the "rubber" match against Joey Maxim in ten rounds at Gilmore Field. Previously, Maxim defeated Walcott in ten rounds on August 28, 1946 in Camden. Walcott avenged his loss with a ten round win on January 6, 1947 in Philadelphia. Later, on December 5 in New York, Walcott lost a fifteen round decision to Heavyweight Champion, Joe Louis. Walcott knocked Louis down twice and probably deserved the win. **(Courtesy Antiquities of the Prize Ring)**

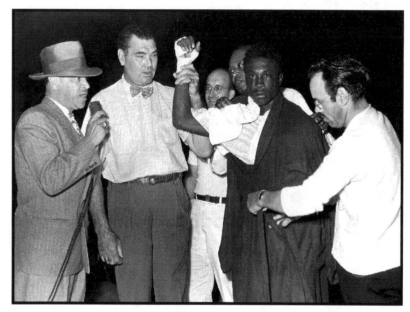

A SHARP HITTING HAND. Former heavyweight great, Jack Dempsey, raises the hand of John L. Davis in victory at the Olympic Auditorium on August 20, 1947. Davis fought primarily in California, including Los Angeles and Hollywood, during his career. He had a good first year, was 9-3-1 in his second year, experienced a tough third year of battles but found himself during his fourth year and put it all together. During the remainder of his career, he gained victories over such men as Sammy Angott, Joe Brown, Harold Jones, Carlos Chavez, Art Aragon, Bernard Docusen and Freddie Dawson. On March 23, 1951, he fought a ten round draw with the talented Eddie Giosa in New York. This was Davis' last bout. He retired from the ring because of a detached retina.

JOEY. "Jolting" Joey Barnum (Guiseppi Mariano Roselli) was a popular glove-tosser around Los Angeles from 1940 to 1952. His career began with an 11-2-3 record but before it was over, he ran into difficulty against the likes of Bob Montgomery, Wesley Mouzon, John Thomas, Aldo Spoldi, Willie Joyce, Enrique Bolanos, Maxie and Bernard Docusen, Del Flanagan and Art Aragon. Joey earned notable victories over Paul Altman, "Spider" Mock (Gene Jensen), Gene Spencer, Johnny Bratton and Eddie Hudson. He was elected to the World Boxing Hall of Fame in 1999.

MARIO. Mario Trigo was a good puncher with a strong left-hook. There was never a dull moment when Trigo fought - and he fought often. In a career that spanned from 1946 through early 1955, Mario engaged in more than 120 bouts and had wins over Bernard Docusen, Art Aragon, Lauro Salas, Carlos Chavez, Rudy Cruz, Jesse Flores, Philip Kim, Joey Barnum, Buddy Jacklich, Ralph Lara, Chuey Figueroa, Eddie Hudson, Fabela Chavez and the former featherweight champion, Jackie Wilson.

UP AND COMING BATTLER. Freddie Beshore, out of Pennsylvania, fought in Los Angeles and Hollywood frequently from 1946 to 1949. Beshore had compiled an 18-2-1 record, including a ten round decision over Ernie Rios, at the time of their second fight, on September 12, 1947 in Hollywood. Beshore hammered Rios down in six rounds in this one and showed a lot of promise.

A PRETTY GOOD MAN. Jackie Blair was a Los Angeles featherweight who began his career in Texas in 1947. After a couple of years, he journeyed to California sporting a 22-2-4 record. During 1949, he earned a 10-4-2 mark. The next year was mediocre and Jackie went 10-6-1. Blair got in gear in 1951, fighting primarily back in Texas, and built a record of 9-3, including wins over Lauro Salas and Manny Ortega. Fighting until 1958, Blair won nearly 90 bouts in his career.

I'LL GET YOU FOR THAT. Eddie Hudson (on the right) lands a blow to the head of tough out-of-towner Buddy Garcia at the Olympic Auditorium on November 4, 1947. Garcia, who had a record of 33-2-1 at the time, came back to score a seventh round knockout over Hudson. Hudson was a scrappy fellow who had a short up-and-down career from 1942-1947. During his career, he managed wins over Bobby Yeager, Johnny Armando, Freddie Long, Don Lemos, Genaro Rojo, Billy George, Cleo Shans, Eddie Marcus and Quentin "Baby" Breese.

GETTING READY. Here, John Thomas is getting some exercise while training for a contest. Thomas was a great attraction for California boxing fans during 1940-1947 and had victories over Henry Armstrong, Willie Joyce, Cleo Shans, Petey Scalzo, Jimmy Doyle, Lew Jenkins, Aldo Spoldi, Tony Chavez, Leo Rodak, Ray Campo, Eddie Marcus and Larry Cisneros. As a lightweight, he was world ranked. Thomas was managed by Bert Lewis and trained by George Tolson. After retiring from the ring, Thomas became involved with California boxing activities and was a popular referee who officiated 21 major world championship bouts held in the Los Angeles area. **(Courtesy Antiquities of the Prize Ring)**

A LOCAL FAVORITE. Ralph Lara (on the right), known as "Little Dynamite," began fighting in Hollywood in 1943 and appeared regularly in Southern California up through 1949. Ralph was a buzz-saw type of fighter who provided some thrilling, action packed fights. He was managed by Canto Robleto and trained by George Leonard. Lara had a good career but never quite reached the upper echelon of lightweights. Here he is shown throwing a right against Maxie Docusen in a losing effort on November 5, 1947 in Oakland.

HOT AND HEAVY AMATEUR ACTION. The Diamond Belt AAU Finals were held at the Hollywood Legion Stadium on November 15, 1947. Sponsored by the Los Angeles Examiner, the event was always a favorite among local boxing fans. A program is shown here. The amateurs really went at it sometimes and this was one of them. The scene is from one of the 1947 Diamond Belt AAU bouts. These two fellows got so tangled up that they took a nosedive through the ropes.

GIVE CREDIT WHERE CREDIT IS DUE.
Shown here is the International Sports Shrine, Helms Hall, in Los Angeles. The Helms Hall Board established many Halls of Fame including Boxing. The Headquarters of the Helms Athletic Foundation was established in 1936 by Bill Schroeder and Paul Helms. Helms Hall was erected in 1948.

HE WAS A CROWD FAVORITE. Hilton "Fitzie" Fitzpatrick shown here with his trainer, Joe Stanley, was born in West Virginia but became a popular fighter in Los Angeles rings during the 1940s. Fitzpatrick, a light heavyweight, came out swinging at the bell. Not a clever boxer but a strong and willing puncher, he came to fight. During his career, Fitzie defeated such men as Pat Valentino, Lee Savold, Rusty Payne, Phil Muscato, Newsboy Millich, Billy Bengal, Jimmy Casino, Watson Jones, "Wild" Bill McDowell and Ernie Rios.

STEPS DOWN. After managing most business affairs at the Hollywood Legion Stadium for sixteen years, Charles MacDonald tendered his resignation, effective February 1, 1948, following serious questions regarding some of his decisions. MacDonald had been relieved of many of his powers following six months of unrest by Legion top management.

MacDonald Plans to Quit Hollywood Legion Fight Job

Charles MacDonald, for 16 years matchmaker and general manager of Hollywood Legion Stadium—next to Madison Square Garden the most famous boxing arena in the nation—will tender his resignation effective Feb. 1, The Times learned exclusively last night.

The action followed six months of unrest and turmoil at the arena, which is operated by Hollywood American Legion Post No. 43. During this time MacDonald has been shorn of some of his powers by a new board which has sought to take over virtual control.

MacDonald's Statement

Contacted late last night, MacDonald admitted he was tendering his resignation.

"Yes," he said, "I'm leaving to go into another business, but first I'm going to take a vacation for a couple of months. The board has not yet acted upon the resignation. My contract has two and one-half years to run, but I have every reason to believe the resignation will be accepted.

"I am leaving with no animosities.

"I wish the post, of which I have been a member for 20 years, and the stadium organization every success in the world."

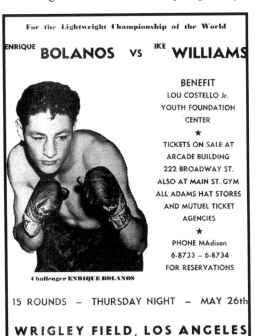

For the Lightweight Championship of the World

ENRIQUE **BOLANOS** vs IKE **WILLIAMS**

BENEFIT
LOU COSTELLO Jr.
YOUTH FOUNDATION
CENTER
★
TICKETS ON SALE AT
ARCADE BUILDING
222 BROADWAY ST.
ALSO AT MAIN ST. GYM
ALL ADAMS HAT STORES
AND MUTUEL TICKET
AGENCIES
★
PHONE MAdison
6-8733 – 6-8734
FOR RESERVATIONS

Challenger ENRIQUE BOLANOS

15 ROUNDS – THURSDAY NIGHT – MAY 26th

WRIGLEY FIELD, LOS ANGELES

GAVE IT A TRY. On April 30, 1946, Enrique Bolanos challenged Ike Williams for the NBA Lightweight title but was stopped in eight rounds. Following the loss, Bolanos proceeded to compile a 20-0-1 mark and on May 25, 1948, tested Williams again for the title (see the flyer to the left - with the wrong date). Williams won a fifteen round decision. Enrique then won nine straight contests before trying Williams a third time on July 21, 1949. This time, Ike stopped Enrique in four rounds. All of these bouts were held at Wrigley Field. **(Courtesy Antiquities of the Prize Ring)**

SOUTHERN TALENT. Bernard Docusen began boxing in 1944, out of New Orleans, and boxed there and in the eastern United States until 1946. Then, he boxed all over the country and appeared in Los Angeles for the first time in 1947, when he decisioned Bobby Yeager and knocked out Joey Barnum. When he began fighting, Bernard lost one bout early in his career and did not lose again until nearly three and a half years later. Then, he won a few more bouts and, sporting 41 wins, met "Sugar" Ray Robinson for the Welterweight Championship on June 28, 1948 in Chicago. Docusen lost in fifteen rounds. Bernard continued to fight after this loss and built an impressive record. In more than 80 bouts, he lost only ten. However, four unfortunate losses that occurred were knockout losses to Freddie Dawson, John L. Davis, Gil Turner and Joey Giambra. **(Courtesy Antiquities of the Prize Ring)**

NICKY BOY. Nick Moran had a career that ran hot-and-cold for ten years. He hit his stride from 1947-1950 and during his tenure in the ring defeated such men as Joey Barnum, Artie Dorrell, Bob Montgomery, Georgie Hansford, Bobby Yeager and "California" Jackie Wilson. **(Courtesy J.J. Johnston)**

L.A. HEAVY. Al Hoosman began fighting in 1940 and did not lose a bout until 1945, when he dropped a decision to Lee Savold. Al redeemed himself immediately with a victory over Savold in his very next fight. Fighting all over the world, Hoosman gained victories over such men as Herb Narvo, Alabama Kid, Bill Poland, Jack "Buddy" Walker, Jerry McSwain, Joe Ray Stevens, Jo Weidin and Tommy Farr.

THE GOOD LOOKING KID. Never a champion but one of the most popular Los Angeles fighters ever, Art "Golden Boy" Aragon first put on his professional gloves in 1944 and posted an 11-1 record for the year. The next year was not good but he roared back in 1946 with all wins except for one draw. Stepping up and getting better during 1947-1948, Art was battling with the best. Come 1949, he emerged as the winner against Harold Jones, Tony Chavez, John L. Davis and Alfredo Escobar. The following year was much the same as he defeated Mario Trigo, Enrique Bolanos and Carlos Chavez.

TOP PROMOTER. Joe Waterman, boxing manager, matchmaker and promoter, passed away on May 5, 1949. According to many, he was the best matchmaker ever in Los Angeles and the West Coast. Waterman was fundamental in bringing many Filipino fighters to California during the 1930s. He served as matchmaker and promoter at the Olympic Auditorium during the mid-late 1930s, made big attractions out of such men as Bob Nestell, Wally Hally, Glen Lee and Henry Armstrong and developed such men as Freddie Steele, Al Hostak and Joe Kahut in Seattle.

VETERAN FIGHT PROMOTER SUCCUMBS

Joe Waterman, 'Savior of Boxing in Los Angeles,' Dies in Tacoma

BY FRANK FINCH

Joe Waterman, once hailed as "the savior of boxing in Los Angeles" for his enterprise in reviving the then moribund mitt game, died yesterday at Tacoma, Wash. A native of Malden, Mass., he was 61.

Cause of his death came from heart attack. Waterman had been afflicted by heart trouble for the past five years.

"Sailor Joe," who earned this sobriquet as a coal-passer in the United States Navy, was nationally known as a boxing manager, matchmaker and promoter.

Developed Cards

As a promoter and matchmaker at the Olympic Auditorium, off and on, from 1935 to 1938, Waterman gave the box office a shot in the arm by building up such colorful local drawing cards as Bob Nestell, Wally Hally, Glen Lee and Henry Armstrong.

Waterman made the match that "made" Armstrong. The tireless Negro was paired with Baby Arizmendi in an outdoor shot at Wrigley Field on Aug. 4, 1936,

with recognition in California as the world's featherweight championship as the stake.

Armstrong dealt Arizmendi a brutal 10-round beating. This victory was the springboard which zoomed Armstrong upwards to ring immortality. He emerged as unchallenged featherweight ruler by stopping the NBA champ, Petey Sarron, and later became the triple titleholder by conquering Welterweight Champ Barney Ross and Lightweight Champ Lou Ambers.

Drew Big Gates

Wherever Sailor Joe hung his hat, the fight game boomed. His magic touch did wonders for the sport in Seattle, Portland, Tacoma and Ocean Park.

With Nate Druxman as his partner in Seattle, Waterman developed Freddie Steele and Al Hostak into middleweight champions.

Portland was a "$500" town when Waterman went to work there. He imported "name" fighters and developed a local topnotcher in Joe Kahut. Soon the boys were being paid off on gates of $10,000 or more.

PASSES — Joe Waterman, veteran ring figure, who died yesterday at Tacoma.

ANOTHER TALENTED SOUTHERNER. Fighting out of New Orleans, Maxie Docusen compiled a wonderful, unbeaten record from 1944 through 1949, winning 61 bouts while drawing three and having one "no contest." During these years, Maxie defeated Alfredo Escobar four times, Joey Barnum three times, Buddy Jacklich three times, Mario Trigo twice, and Carlos Chavez, John L. Davis, Manuel Ortiz, Enrique Bolanos, Tony Chavez and Jackie Weber once each. During 1950, he lost three fights while winning only two, signaling a decline in his performance. In his entire career of more than 80 bouts, he lost only six times. Maxie fought in the Los Angeles area on twenty-one occasions. **(Courtesy Antiquities of the Prize Ring)**

A TOP FIGHTER. Rudolpho "Rudy" Cruz began his career in 1943 and racked up 9 wins before losing for the first time to Chuey Figoerua. Following this setback, Cruz won nineteen battles and improved his record to 28-1. Then, he lost four straight bouts to Ike Williams, Eddie Giosa and Tommy Campbell, twice. Rudy won nine of his next twelve. Cruz retired from boxing in 1952 after capturing nine wins in his last 11 bouts.

MILO, THE SAVAGE. Milo Savage was a boxer for 25 years, from November of 1945 through July of 1970, and engaged in more than 100 bouts. He began fighting in the northwest and fought in California and across the United States. He also had bouts in Australia. Savage scored wins over Frankie Angustain, Bobby Boyd, Al "Tiger" Williams, Holly Mims, Esau Ferdinand, Jack Snapp, Charlie Sawyer and Neal Rivers. He also had draws with Kenny Watkins, Eduardo Lausse, Willie Vaughn and Jimmy Brooks.

GOOD START, BAD ENDING. Frankie Daniels began fighting in 1948 and had a lengthy career that lasted into 1964. By late 1949, he had built a fine 11-0-1 record. Then, he met "Irish" Bob Murphy and suffered his first defeat. After this loss, Daniels had a so-so career up to 1959 when he pulled off a win over Bob Baker. From that point on, Daniels won just 3 of his last 24 bouts in the ring.

ANOTHER SALAS. Charley Salas had a lengthy and excellent career in the ring. Hailing from Phoenix, Arizona, Charley fought in the Los Angeles area on many occasions. Salas gained his first big win in 1946 over Flash Gordon in San Diego. Before he hung up the gloves, he had victories over Ike Williams, Willie Vaughn, Bobby Yeager, "California" Jackie Wilson, Shamus McCray, Tony Chavez, Bobby Lakin, Freddie "Babe" Herman, Jimmy Hatcher, Charley "Red" Williams, Ray Brown, John L. Davis, Elmer Beltz, Joey Barnum, Bobby Jones, Eusebio "Chebo" Hernandez, Jesse Turner, Livio Minelli, Chico Varona and Georgie Johnson. **(Courtesy J.J. Johnston)**

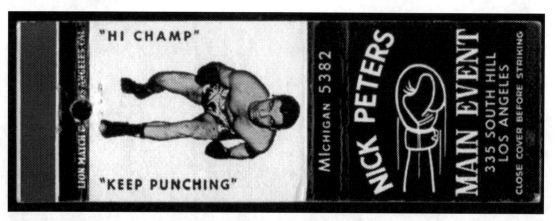

FAMOUS RESTAURANT. Nick "the Greek" Peters had his first fight in the Los Angeles area against Davey Abad in 1937 and from then until the end of his career, he appeared frequently in Hollywood. During his career, Peters defeated such men as Wally Hally, Georgie Hansford, Mike Belloise, Joey Ferrando and Johnny Rohrig. Nick's *Main Event* restaurant was a popular hangout for many boxing people during the 1940s and 1950s. Shown here is a matchbook cover that publicizes his place and contains a photo image of Peters.

HAPPY BIRTHDAY. Old Jim Jeffries was touched when many long-time friends gathered at his home in Burbank on April 15, 1950 to celebrate his seventy-fifth birthday. Shown here are four of them. From left to right are Nat Fleischer (Editor of *The Ring* magazine), Jerry Geisler (former California State Boxing Commissioner), Jeffries, Dan Long (76 year old policeman friend who boxed Jeffries in Jim's third ring fight) and Dan McLeod (former heavyweight wrestling champion).

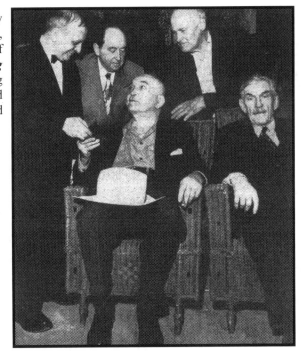

FEARLESS BABE. Freddie "Babe" Herman was a talented fighter whose career lasted from 1946 to 1957. Herman engaged in more than 100 contests and fought many top contenders. After an outstanding start of 16-1-1, his record had its ups-and-downs. During his early career, he had wins over Lou Filippo, Darnell Carter and Ernie Hunick. At the top of his game in 1949 and 1950, when he was fighting the best around, he gained victories over Philip Kim, Harold Jones and Johnny Forte. Later, he posted wins over Nick Moran, Mario Trigo, Joe Felan and Archie Whitewater.

QUITE A HITTER. Clarence Henry (on the right) knocked Johnny Holman down in the eighth round of their bout at the Olympic Auditorium on June 13, 1950 and went on to win a ten round decision. Henry was born in San Antonio, Texas but fought out of Los Angeles. Fighting mostly between 183 and 188 pounds, he was rather light for fighting in the heavyweight division but nevertheless was a fierce competitor. During his first four years, he built a 30-2-1 record with one "no contest" bout. His only losses during these years came against the great Jimmy Bivins and the more experienced Frankie Buford. **(Courtesy Clay Moyle)**

THE BEGINNING OF THE END. Art Aragon (on the left) floors Enrique Bolanos in the third round of their July 18, 1950 bout en route to a TKO victory. This was the second stoppage in 1950 for Aragon against the old veteran of the ring who was on a downward spiral in his career. The first match took place on February 14. Each bout was held at the Olympic Auditorium and Mushy Callahan refereed each contest.

A HARD HITTING IRISHMAN. "Irish" Bob Murphy (Edwin Lee O'Connerty), above right, poses with Jimmy Beau prior to their December 8, 1950 bout in New York, won by Murphy in seven rounds. A man with a real punch, "Irish" Bob was born in Flagler, Colorado and appeared in the Los Angeles area twenty times during his career. He won the Light Heavyweight Championship of California in 1950. A southpaw, Bob won 65 of his 78 bouts and scored 56 knockouts. A top title contender, he scored victories over such men as Lloyd Marshall, Danny Nardico, Jake LaMotta and Dan Bucceroni.

ANOTHER GOOD MAN. Fabela Chavez, right, shown here with his manager, George Parnassus, was a very good featherweight out of Hollywood who fought from the mid-1940s into the mid-1950s. Reportedly, he had more than 170 amateur fights. During his career, Fabela earned victories over such men as Art Aragon, Alfredo Escobar, Mario Trigo, Bobby Bell and Harold Dade. On June 29, 1951, he boxed a twelve round draw with Lauro Salas. This was the first of three bouts held in Hollywood against Salas. One month later, on July 27, he defeated Salas in twelve rounds to win the Featherweight Championship of California. After defeating Javier "Baby Face" Gutierrez, Chavez once again fought Lauro Salas for the California Featherweight title. In this contest, held on September 28, he was stopped in the twelfth round and lost the title to Salas.

ANOTHER SLICK ONE. Elmer Beltz had a short career, from 1948-1953, but a good one. He lost only four bouts during his first five years. Beltz posted wins over Flash Gordon, Archie Whitewater, Freddie "Babe" Herman, Joey Carkido, Gus "Pell" Mell, Walter Haines and Benny Black. He also fought draws with Jesse Flores, Vic Cardell and Willie Pastrano.

LOS ANGELES OLYMPIC AUD. MAY 8, 1951

IN defeating Mario Trigo at the Los Angeles Olympic, Art Aragon won the California lightweight title and the dubious distinction of being the foremost contender (California version) for world title. And some of the local scribes stated that he looked the part. Personally, I thought that Art made one of his poorest fights, even though he did stop Trigo—with Referee Charlie Randolph's assistance—in the 9th heat.

It was an action scrap and although not one-sided, Trigo was the recipient of much punishment. Mario was not as elusive as usual, in fact, was an easy target, but, due to poor timing, Aragon missed half his punches. Aragon, set on a kayo victory, stalked Trigo continually and had his jinx opponent hurt and wobbly several times, but couldn't put over a finisher. Trigo appeared about to cave in numerous times, but he recuperates quickly, and would always come back with a counter attack. Mario was decked once, a short hook dropping him for a 1-count in the second.

Trigo outslugged the tired Aragon in the 8th, and came out fast in the 9th, forcing Art to give ground but shortly after was knocked into the ropes from a left hook to the jaw. Seeing his foe was hurt, Aragon tore in with a vengeance, raining lefts and rights to Mario's head. Trigo was being badly pounded but appeared in no worse shape than on several previous occasions and the referee's action in halting the fight at this point brought forth considerable booing.

ARAGON WINS. To the left is newspaper coverage of Art Aragon's victory over Mario Trigo at the Olympic Auditorium on May 8, 1951, when he won the California Lightweight title. In it, he is called the foremost contender for the world title. Aragon peaked in 1951 when he won his first six bouts of the year including a decision over Champion Jimmy Carter in a non-title bout. Then, he met Carter for the Lightweight Championship on November 14, 1951 at the Olympic Auditorium, but lost in 15 rounds.

PULLED IT OFF. Art Aragon rests his head on the ropes after coming on strong in the late rounds and winning a split decision in a non-title fight against Lightweight Champion Jimmy Carter on August 28, 1951. Carter gained revenge three months later in a title contest. A third bout was fought between the two in 1956. Aragon won that one. All three bouts were held at the Olympic Auditorium.

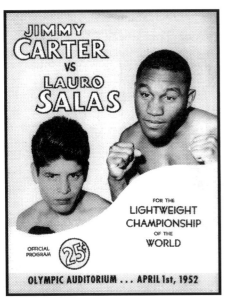

JIMMY
CARTER
VS
LAURO
SALAS

OFFICIAL PROGRAM

FOR THE
LIGHTWEIGHT
CHAMPIONSHIP
OF THE
WORLD

25

OLYMPIC AUDITORIUM ... APRIL 1st, 1952

PROGRAM FOR A CARTER-SALAS BOUT. On April 1, 1952, Jimmy Carter defeated Lauro Salas in fifteen rounds at the Olympic Auditorium to retain his Lightweight Championship. Shown here is a program for the bout. In a rematch, Salas avenged the loss on May 14 at the Olympic and took the crown. **(Courtesy Antiquities of the Prize Ring)**

THE CHILLER. Charley "Chiller" Green was a good punching fighter who captured the Middleweight Championship of California during his career. His peak time was during 1951-1954 when he posted a 23-4 streak with victories over such men as Johnny Duke, Art Soto, Esau Ferdinand, Watson Jones, Willie Vaughn, Milo Savage and Sal Flores.

KEENY. Ignacio "Keeny" Teran was a shrewd, sharp-shooting flyweight who appeared in Los Angeles and Hollywood from 1951-1955 and built a nifty 25-4-1 record with wins over Tommy Umeda, Bobby Garza, Johnny Ortega and Henry "Pappy" Gault and a draw with Gil Cadilli.

WORLD FAMOUS. Tommy Harrison (on the right), Los Angeles light heavyweight and heavyweight, takes a swipe at Ezzard Charles in their 1953 battle that Charles won. Harrison met the best during his career that lasted from 1951 to 1958. He fought 25 contests during his first two years. In his career, he gained wins over such men as Jimmy Bivins twice, Wes Bascom twice, Charley Norkus and Paul Andrews. His six battles with Frankie Crane at the Olympic Auditorium and Hollywood Legion Stadium were treats for local fans. Following his 1953 loss to Charles, his career took a downward turn. Tommy fought sparingly during 1954-1958.

GABRIEL "HAP" NAVARRO. "Hap" was born in Los Angeles, near the Olympic Auditorium, in 1919. He joined the Hollywood American Legion Stadium staff as a publicity man in 1948, rose to become Assistant Matchmaker in 1950 and head Matchmaker in 1953, replacing Cal Working. His tenure at the Legion club was brief but eventfully successful. He won the award for "Best Fight of the Year" in 1954 when he matched Jackie McCoy's protégé Buddy Evatt against Andy Escobar. In 1956, he broke the gate receipts mark for the club by matching World Middleweight Champion "Bobo" Olson against California Champion Willie Vaughn. During his stay in Hollywood, "Hap" broke the existing record for gate receipts of a televised fight at the club seven times. He resigned in 1955 to enter private business as a publicist but two of his bouts were still nominated for best fight of the year in his absence. He also made matches for the Bakersfield Arena, the Mexicali Bull Ring and the Albuquerque American Legion Armory. Now, semi-retired, he lives with his family in San Diego. This photo was taken by Otto Jensen of Hollywood. **(Courtesy "Hap" Navarro)**

LOST BY CUTS. Davey Gallardo started boxing in 1948 and waged most of his campaigns in Los Angeles. He was a good fighter but slipped up from time to time. From 1948-1951, he posted a 33-11-5 mark. His best year was 1952, when he compiled eleven wins against no defeats or draws and won the California Featherweight title over Al Cruz in twelve rounds at the Olympic Auditorium. Here, Gallardo (on the right) traveled to Madison Square Garden and tangled with Lulu Perez on September 4, 1953. Davey came out on the short end when a serious cut was sustained near his left eye and the bout was stopped.

SELECT COMPANY. At a dinner on Olvera Street honoring Cisco Andrade in 1953, "Hap" Navarro (seated, left) and his lovely wife, Jo, are joined by John Hall (standing, left) of the Los Angeles Mirror-Times and Rudy Garcia, sports editor of the Spanish language daily "La Opinion." Navarro handled the "Bobo" Olson camp for the record-breaking Wrigley Field match with "Sugar" Ray Robinson in 1956. He also headed the publicity department for the "Bobo" Olson vs. Joey Giambra contest at the Cow Palace in San Francisco, also in 1956. **(Courtesy "Hap" Navarro)**

CARNIVAL. Henry Armstrong (center, pulling the bar) is supplying the muscle in the gym before a collection of ring greats. The fellows were conditioning themselves for the Carnival of Champions show to be held in Los Angeles in September of 1953. It was an effort to help fund the Henry Armstrong Youth Foundation's *Boys' Town* Camp to be located in San Fernando Valley. Left to right are Alberto "Baby" Arizmendi, Barney Ross, Armstrong, Fidel LaBarba and Jimmy McLarnin.

THE WILDCAT. Philip Kim was a fine welterweight who began his fighting in Honolulu in 1947 and racked up a 28-5-2 record before fighting actively in the Los Angles area in 1952 and 1953. Among the victims in his ring career were Archie Whitewater, Freddie "Babe" Herman, Mario Trigo, Manny Madrid, Bobby Terrance, Elmer Beltz, Virgil Akins and Carlos Chavez.

SCRAPPY WELTERWEIGHT. Ramon Fuentes built up a 25-3 record during 1950-1953, including wins over Charley Salas, Phil Burton, Bobby Jones and Mario Trigo. He picked up the California Welterweight title along the way. Then, following two losses – to Kid Gavilan and Gil Turner - Fuentes pulled off a big upset when he defeated Art Aragon in ten rounds on October 2, 1953. He added wins over Art Soto, Carmine Fiore, Billy Graham and Ernie Greer in 1954 and boosted his record to 31-4 by the year's end. Over the next few years, Fuentes was a top welterweight and defeated such men as George Barnes, Joe Miceli, Chico Vejar and Kid Gavilan. He also fought a draw with Gil Turner.

UP-AND-DOWN CAREER. Willie Bean was a heavyweight who fought out of Los Angeles from 1946-1956. Bean had an up-and-down career that peaked during 1948-1950. During this time, Willie had earned victories over Jerry McSwain, George "Baby Dutch" Culbertson, Billy Gilliam, Ted Lowry, Al Hoosman, Frankie Buford and Rusty Payne. Bean continued his career, showing promise from time to time, and gained wins over Bill Petersen, Pat Comiskey, Albert "Turkey" Thompson, Frankie Daniels, Howard King, Dave Whitlock, Hank Thurman, Jesse Hall and Dale Hall. During his career, Bean was the Heavyweight Champion of California. **(Courtesy J.J. Johnston)**

FIGHTER, REFEREE, JUDGE. Lou Filippo was a boxer from the late 1940s until the late 1950s. During his career, he defeated such men as Darnell Carter, Johnny Hart, Gilberto Muniz, Rudy Mendoza, Vince Bonomo, Art Ramponi, Tommy Vargas and Bernardo Ramirez. After his fighting days were over, Lou became a referee and judge, primarily in the Southern California area. He also appeared as a referee or judge in the *Rocky* movie series. As a fitting conclusion to a fine career devoted to boxing, Filippo has served as an executive of the World Boxing Hall of Fame. **(Courtesy J.J. Johnston)**

WILLIE, MEET HAP. Willie Vaughn (on the left) was a scrappy fighter who waged ring wars as a middleweight in the area during the 1950s. Here, Willie shakes hands with "Hap" Navarro, outstanding matchmaker at the Hollywood American Legion Stadium. Vaughn's career peaked during 1953-1957 as he compiled a 24-11-4 record against many of the best men in the world and owned wins over such men as Earl Turner, Charley "Chiller" Green, Esau Ferdinand, Jimmy Morris, Sal Perea, Garth Panter, Al "Tiger" Williams, Charley Joseph, Felix Benson and Ralph "Tiger" Jones. During his career, Vaughn was the Middleweight Champion of California. **(Courtesy "Hap" Navarro)**

WELTERWEIGHT WARRIOR. From June of 1950 until April of 1954, Charley Sawyer lost only a couple of bouts. In his career, Sawyer achieved victories over such men as Cisco Saenz, Baby Ike, Earl Turner, Charley "Tombstone" Smith, Pat Manzi, Virgil Akins and Gerald Gray. In 1959, at the Hollywood Legion Stadium, he met Art Aragon in a match that was called a knockout for Aragon but afterwards questioned as a fake.

VERY GOOD BOXER. Ramon Tiscareno fought from 1949 to 1958 and was among the best in the welterweight division. During his tenure in the ring, Ramon took the measure of Archie Whitewater, Freddie "Babe" Herman, Santiago Esteban, Joe Fisher, Bill Sudduth, Mario Trigo, Art Soto, Philip Kim, Carlos Chavez and Henry Davis. Two of his losses were to Art Aragon in 1956 and Vince Martinez in 1957.

HE'S OUT. Carl "Bobo" Olson is down in his last Middleweight title bout against "Sugar" Ray Robinson. This contest was held on May 18, 1956 at Wrigley Field. It was Olson's fourth loss to Robinson in title fights, three by knockout. They never fought again. Olson decided he had enough "Sugar" for one career. Referee "Mushy" Callahan is directing Robinson to a neutral corner.

END OF THE ROAD. The activities of "Babe" McCoy were investigated during 1956 by a special committee appointed by the California, Governor Goodwin Knight. A number of boxers testified that "Babe" had "fixed" bouts they were involved in. Among those speaking out were Watson Jones, Carlos Chavez, Tommy Campbell, Georgie Hansford, Ira "Pinky" Hughes, "Young" Harry Wills and James "Tiger" Sheppard. McCoy was not prosecuted because several years had passed since the illegal proceedings had taken place. But, he was barred from boxing activities in the state of California and never again did he promote a bout. Al McCoy, older brother and former Middleweight Champion, was extremely displeased with "Babe" over these fixes and quite outspoken in his disgust.

GIL WAS GOOD. Gil Cadilli was a talented featherweight who fought from 1950-1963. During his first four years, he earned 17 wins with only one loss and two draws. Gil defeated such men as Jackie Blair, Fabela Chavez, Luis Castillo, Willie Pep, Rudy Garcia, Ike Chestnut and Danny Valdez. Cadilli was the Featherweight Champion of California during his career.

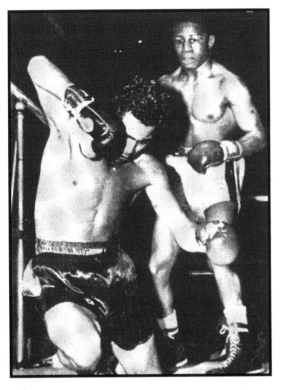

SWEET PEA. Here, Billy "Sweet Pea" Peacock downs Raul "Raton" Macias. Peacock fought as a bantamweight from 1951 until 1961 and had two streaks where he was among the best. From 1951-1953, he had a 19-3 record and from 1955 through early 1957 he posted a 15-2-1 mark. Billy defeated such men as Henry "Pappy" Gault, Pierre "Cosse" Cossemyns, Ignacio "Keeny" Teran, Raul "Raton" Macias, Alex Fimbres, Vic Eisen, Jose "Toluco" Lopez and Rudy Garcia. Billy was the Bantamweight Champion of California and North America during his tenure in the ring.

BIG BOB. Bob Albright (on the right) is seen here in one of his battles against Ezzard Charles. Bob began his heavyweight career with a very good 17-1-1 record during 1953-1954. As he stepped up in competition, wins were harder to get as he fought the very best men available – Ezzard Charles, Howard King, Cleveland Williams, Archie Moore and Pat McMurtry. During his career, Bob beat such men as Keene Simmons, Johnny Arthur, Joey Rowan, Clarence Williams and Regan "Buddy" Turman.

MR. JORDAN, SIR. Rudy Jordan was a successful lightweight fighter during the 1950s and owned victories over the best – Jimmy Carter, Carlos Chavez, Lou Filippo, Teddy "Red Top" Davis, Manuel Castillo, Art Ramponi, Mickey Northrup and Tommy Romulo. After his fighting days were over, Rudy went on to become a highly successful referee and judge. During his career, he refereed 13 major world title bouts in the Los Angeles area and earned his way into the World Boxing Hall of Fame.

YOUNG JACK JOHNSON. Johnson (John Lee Story), who had an up-and-down career, was active from 1953-1963. During this time, he was the Heavyweight Champion of California and defeated such men as Willie Bean, Marty Marshall, Zora Folley, Ezzard Charles, Duke Sabedong, Willi Besmanoff, George Logan and Sonny Banks. Johnson met an untimely death in the fall of 1963, when he was fatally stabbed by his step-daughter at his home in Queens, New York. **(Courtesy J.J. Johnston)**

CALIFORNIA FEATHER CHAMP. Tommy Bain (on the left), posing with comedian, Lou Costello, hailed from Indianapolis and built a fine 25-3-2 record by the time he came to the area in 1955. Tommy fought mainly in Hollywood and racked up four victories before fighting Kenny Davis for the California Featherweight title on August 11, 1956. Stopping Davis in the sixth round, Bain afterwards experienced some tough times, losing the next five bouts. Then, he went 3-3 to finish out his career, losing his California Featherweight crown in the process.

Chapter Six

The Aileen Eaton and George Parnassus Era

1956-1980

After "Babe" McCoy resigned as the matchmaker of the Olympic Auditorium in 1956, Cal Working replaced him. Working made way a short time later for George Parnassus, who became the matchmaker on July 8, 1957.

With George Parnassus matching them up, the Olympic Boxing Club continued to have much success. Parnassus was another of the long line of Olympic Auditorium matchmakers who had considerable experience as a boxing man, in particular, as the manager of World Middleweight Champion, Ceferino Garcia, and the popular lightweight contender, Enrique Bolanos. While he was a matchmaker and a promoter, he brought in many top fighters boxers from Mexico to headline major boxing cards in Los Angeles. Mexican boxers such as Raul "Raton" Macias, Ricardo "Pajarito" Moreno, Jose Becerra, Raymundo "Battling" Torres, Ruben Olivares, Carlos Zarate and Jose "Pipino" Cuevas drew huge gates in the Los Angeles area over the next twenty-five years.

During the latter part of the 1950s, the number of boxing clubs and shows declined in all parts of the United States. The Los Angeles area was not immune to the trend. The Ocean Park Arena presented its last boxing show in 1957. The largest blow of the period came when the fabled Hollywood Legion Stadium closed its doors in 1959 after being the venue for boxing cards since 1921. The Legion Stadium was converted into a bowling alley.

However, the Los Angeles area was more resistant to the decline in clubs and shows than other metropolitan areas in the United States due largely to the devout Mexican and Mexican-American boxing fans. In fact, many major boxing shows staged in the Los Angeles area continued to draw large and enthusiastic crowds during the second half of the Twentieth Century. The Olympic Auditorium was the site for weekly boxing shows until the early 1980s, well over fifty-five years after it opened. This is an incredible record due to the fact that there were few clubs staging weekly cards in the United States at this time.

Wrigley Field continued to be the site of many major bouts during most of the 1950s but this changed in the latter part of the decade. During the late 1950s, the Los Angeles Sports Arena opened for business and was the venue for a number of boxing cards over a span of several decades. With a capacity of over fifteen thousand, the Sports Arena was the first in-door sports facility in Los Angeles that was close to being on par with the Olympia in Detroit, Chicago Stadium, Boston Garden and Madison Square Garden.

The Los Angeles Memorial Coliseum, with its capacity of about 100,000, replaced Wrigley Field as a boxing venue for outdoor boxing shows in the early 1960s with the exception of one boxing show in Dodger Stadium (capacity of 56,000) in 1963. The Memorial Coliseum staged its last boxing show during the early 1970s.

Jackie Leonard, the last matchmaker in the Hollywood Legion Stadium, was in the news often during the late 1950s and the early 1960s. Besides the difficulties of presenting boxing cards in the famed venue, Leonard was involved with some of the most powerful boxing figures of the time who were implicated in an attempt to forcibly share in the earnings of a World Welterweight Champion, Don Jordan. Those implicated were Frankie Carbo, a reputed mobster who was regarded as the boss of boxing and controlled a number of the best-known fighters for close to two decades; Frank "Blinky" Palermo, another reputed mobster who managed a lot of well-known boxers during the 1940s and 1950s; Truman Gibson, a black man who was the secretary of the International Boxing Corporation, the most powerful boxing promotion organization in the United States during the 1950s; Louis Tom Dragna, a reputed hoodlum; and Joe Sica, another reputed hoodlum.

In a federal court in Los Angeles on May 31, 1961, Carbo, Palermo, Gibson and Sica were convicted of conspiracy and extortion charges in connection with the attempt to take over the management of Jordan. Leonard and Don Nesseth, the manager of Jordan, were considered the main witnesses in the three-month trial presided over by Judge Ernest A. Tolin. Alvin H. Goldstein, special assistant to the United States Attorney General, Robert Kennedy, led the prosecution. A jury of ten women and two men rendered the verdict. Goldstein said, "This is one of the few cases ever tried which reaches the heart of underworld activities."

Since Tolin, the presiding judge, died soon after convictions, Judge George Boldt filled in and sentenced the convicted defendants in December 1961. Carbo was given twenty-five years in prison; Palermo, fifteen years; and Sica, twenty years. Gibson was placed on five-year probation after getting a suspended sentence of five years. In addition, all four men were fined ten thousand dollars each. Although Dragna wasn't fined, he was sentenced to five years for each count, to be served concurrently.

The Olympic Boxing Club had success despite the presence of the Dodgers (professional baseball), Lakers (professional basketball) and Rams (professional football) in competition for the sports dollar. In fact, 1960 proved to be a huge year for the club. The club staged an astounding seventy-six boxing cards, including six World Title bouts. Two of the world title bouts were on the club's biggest show featuring Jose Becerra vs. Alphonse Halimi and Carlos Ortiz vs. "Battling" Torres in the Memorial Coliseum and drew a then-record California gate of $383,331. Also, in 1960, another Olympic Club show featured a World Middleweight title bout between Gene Fullmer and "Sugar" Ray Robinson in the Sports Arena. Pone Kingpetch, Eder Jofre and Joe Brown were other champions featured in World Title bouts staged in the Olympic Auditorium.

During 1963 in Dodger Stadium, World Featherweight Champion, Davey Moore, lost his title to Ultiminio "Sugar" Ramos and sustained fatal injuries. Following the death of Moore, there was no more boxing staged in the facility, leaving the Memorial Coliseum as the main outdoor facility for large boxing events.

In 1963, a slump in attendance in regular boxing cards took place in the Olympic Auditorium. As a result, beginning on February 4, 1964, the Olympic Boxing Club held its regular shows in the Valley Garden Arena in North Hollywood rather than the Olympic Auditorium. But, the move proved to be short-lived. As of October 23, 1964, the club had staged only sixteen boxing shows, eight of which netted less than $2,000.

In 1965, Mickey Davies took over from George Parnassus as the matchmaker of the Olympic Boxing Club. Davies' stint proved to be very successful. In an attempt to increase interest in boxing, there were weekly telecasts of boxing programs starting on May 20, 1965. Davies and a young sportscaster named Dick Enberg were the commentators for the telecasts on the local television station, KTLA. For the big shows in the Olympic Auditorium, only the under-card was shown on television in order to increase the live gate. Enberg went on to be a nationally famous sportscaster in a career that lasted into the 21st Century.

After Cal Eaton died in 1966, Aileen Eaton was regarded as the sole promoter of boxing cards staged by the Olympic Boxing Club. In the middle 1960s, there was an impressive new crop of young popular fighters such as Jerry Quarry, Armando "Mando" Ramos, Raul Rojas, Rodolfo Gonzales, Frankie Crawford and Ruben Navarro, who appeared on cards promoted by the club during the next few years. The biggest draw for Eaton during this period was Armando "Mando" Ramos, a colorful Mexican-American fighter who had much success as a teenager under the management of Jackie McCoy, a legendary boxing figure in the area. Ramos won the World Lightweight title at the age of 20 and the WBC version of the same title at the age of 23. However, his career ended at the age of 26, following three years of declining performances.

In the late 1960s, Jack Kent Cooke, owner of the Lakers at the time, was awarded a franchise in the National Hockey League, when it expanded from six teams to twelve. Due to a business squabble, Cooke built a new arena in Inglewood, called the Forum, with a capacity of around 18,000. Later, it was called the Great Western Forum, named after a large savings and loan company. The Forum staged more boxing shows over the next three decades than any other venue in the area, with the possible exception of the Olympic Auditorium. In addition, starting in 1967, both the Lakers and the new hockey team, the Kings, played their home games there for a little over thirty years.

With George Parnassus acting as the promoter, the Forum became a venue of spectacular boxing shows seen by large crowds during the late 1960s and early 1970s. During that period, Parnassus's biggest draw was Ruben Olivares, a hard-hitting Mexican boxer, who became an all-time great and won World Championships in both the bantamweight and the featherweight divisions.

Another drawing card for Parnassus was Jose Napoles, a Cuban exile who moved to Mexico. Napoles was a boxer with magnificent skill and plenty of power. He was an all-time great and won the World Welterweight Championship two times. By the late 1960s, there was no question that the success of boxing shows in the Los Angeles area was very dependent upon fans of Mexican descent.

Mexican fighters generally were the most popular among crowds in the area, even more popular than Mexican-American fighters. As a result, many fight crowds chanted "Mexico! Mexico! Mexico!" during bouts that involved Mexican fighters. It was evident that boxing fans of Mexican descent were among the most passionate in the world.

Both the Olympic and Forum Boxing Clubs staged televised boxing cards weekly during the early 1970s. Often, the Forum Boxing Club presented cards in other venues in the area besides the Forum. Eventually, the Forum ceased staging cards on a weekly basis, which left the Olympic Auditorium as the sole venue doing so.

By the middle 1970s, most of the weekly shows in the Olympic Auditorium drew only a few thousand people. For these shows, a general admission ticket was only three dollars. During this time, the Olympic was in poor condition and the surrounding neighborhood became worse. Still, many boxing fans felt the Olympic was the best place to see a boxing card because it was built with only boxing in mind, unlike the utility arenas such as the Great Western Forum and Sports Arena.

During the 1970s, there appeared a new crop of exciting young fighters, including Carlos Zarate, Carlos Palomino, Armando Muniz, Bobby Chacon, Danny "Little Red" Lopez, Alfonso Zamora, Jose "Pipino" Cuevas and Guadalupe "Lupe" Pintor. Each fighter engaged in thrilling bouts and, with the exception of Muniz, all of these fighters became World Champions. However, only Zarate went on to become an all-time great during a brilliant career, mostly in the bantamweight division.

With his thrilling style and a booming left hook, "Pipino" Cuevas succeeded Ruben Olivares as the most popular fighter among area fans. Even when he faced a mediocre opponent, enthusiastic fans turned out to see him in action.

Interest in boxing picked up in the middle 1970s. All three major television networks, CBS, ABC and NBC, showed many bouts on television. This upsurge was partly due to the comeback of Muhammad Ali early in the decade. His major bouts were shown on closed circuit telecasts while his minor ones were available on regular television. Also, the excellent performance by the United States boxing team in the 1976 Olympics in Montreal increased the major networks' interest in boxing. As a result, purses for the top smaller boxers skyrocketed.

Prior to the middle 1970s, many important bouts were staged in Los Angeles because of the large crowds and gates generated there. But, with major television money, the live gates became less important. Casinos in Las Vegas and, later on, Atlantic City paid huge site fees for major bouts.

Further, the major networks did not want to black out telecasts in major markets. This made gambling resorts like Las Vegas and Atlantic City even more attractive. Consequently, Los Angeles had fewer major bouts.

Despite the fact that many important bouts were staged in Las Vegas and Atlantic City, there were a number of boxing shows in the Los Angeles area after the middle 1970s. But, there were relatively few large crowds or gates for such shows.

YOU CAN DO IT. Cisco Andrade is shown here getting some advice from a popular fan of his, Frank Sinatra. Cisco had an outstanding career and was unbeaten with a 27-0-1 record during his first three years of fighting. Andrade gave center stage a try in Hollywood and Los Angeles on numerous occasions. Victories over Carlos Chavez, Lauro Salas, Wallace "Bud" Smith and Raymundo "Battling" Torres were standout wins. On August 29, 1956 in Wrigley Field, he had the popular Art Aragon cut over both eyes and bleeding from the nose and mouth. But, the "Golden Boy" rallied and stopped Andrade in the ninth round. Cisco was back at the Olympic Auditorium on October 28, 1960 in an attempt to capture the Lightweight crown from Joe Brown but lost in fifteen rounds. **(Courtesy Antiquities of the Prize Ring)**

SOMEBODY UP THERE. In a great 1956 movie about Middleweight Champion Rocky Graziano, *Somebody Up There Likes Me,* Hollywood continued its fascination with boxing. Shown here, Graziano (Paul Newman) pushes the baby carriage with his fiancée (Pier Angeli) in the midst of an admiring public.

THE KEED WINS AGAIN. In seventh round action, Kid Gavilan (facing the camera) throws a left and cocks his right for a follow-up blow against Chico Vejar in the Olympic Auditorium on November 13, 1956. Gavilan won a ten round decision. The referee was Mushy Callahan. **(Courtesy HERALD-EXAMINER COLLECTION / Los Angeles Public Library)**

FRIENDLY GET TOGETHER. Tony Anthony (left) serves some delicacies to Archie Moore (center) and Ricardo "Pajarito" Moreno in a pre-fight gathering. Moreno (right) seems to be lecturing the fellows on watching their weights. Moore (Archibald Lee Wright) successfully defended his Light-Heavyweight Championship by stopping Anthony in seven rounds in the Olympic Auditorium on September 20, 1957. Moore was one of the legends of the ring, fighting for 29 years, engaging in more than 215 bouts, and scoring 132 knockouts (reports vary). The "Mongoose" was a clever boxer and a stiff hitter. He attempted on two occasions to win the World Heavyweight Championship but was unsuccessful.

ARABIC KING. Alphonse Halimi successfully defended his Bantamweight Championship of the World at Wrigley Field on November 6, 1957 against Raul "Raton" Macias by winning a fifteen round decision. It was another great program put on by Cal Eaton.

PAJARITO HAMMERS HIS WAY TO VICTORY. Above, "Pajarito" Moreno (on the left) batters Ike Chestnut on the way to a sixth round knockout in their November 21, 1957 bout in the Olympic Auditorium. This win set up a title shot for Moreno, who was a favorite among boxing fans in southern California. "Pajarito" was a murderous puncher, scoring 59 knockouts in his 73 fights.

BASSEY KEEPS HIS TITLE. In the photo to the right, on April 1, 1958, Hogan "Kid" Bassey (on the left) visited Wrigley Field and knocked out "Pajarito" Moreno in three rounds in defense of his Featherweight Championship. Bassey was able to offset Moreno's devastating punches with his quickness, boxing and punching – a combination that proved to be a winner.

BOOTSIE. Horace "Boots" Monroe boxed out of Hollywood from 1957 to 1963 and was an outstanding bantamweight and featherweight. He was ranked as high as the #7 bantamweight in the world during 1958 and 1959. Monroe won the Bantamweight Championship of California in 1958 by defeating Billy Peacock.

A BIG FIGHT. Below right, on August 18, 1958, Floyd Patterson defended his Heavyweight Championship at Wrigley Field against Roy "Cut-And-Shoot" Harris, from the Lone Star State. Patterson boasted a 33-1 record, with 24 knockouts, at the time. Harris had a mark of 23-0 and 9 knockouts. Patterson stopped Harris in thirteen rounds. Little did fans know that this would be the last World Heavyweight title fight in California for forty-five years. The referee was "Mushy" Callahan. William "Bill" Paul Rosensohn, a capable young entrepreneur, was the man who made it possible for Los Angeles to host this bout. Rosensohn was a pioneer in theater television, having brought Notre Dame football games to movie-goers in 1953. Bill promoted the Patterson-Harris contest in his first effort at producing major fights. When local boxing authorities turned down Al Weill as promoter, Rosensohn stepped forward and offered to handle the endeavor himself.

CALIFORNIA BOY. Don Jordan was actively promoted by "Babe" McCoy as an up-and-coming champion. Jordan didn't let him down. Don's career started off in a blaze, going 23-4 in the first three years. Then, it was up-down until he hit full stride in March of 1957. From then until late 1959, he compiled a 21-2 mark. Along the way, on December 5, 1958, Jordan defeated Virgil Akins in fifteen rounds at the Olympic Auditorium for the Welterweight crown. Afterwards, he gained another title win over Akins and a successful title defense against Denny Moyer. Jordan lost his crown to Benny "Kid" Paret in 1960. **(Courtesy Antiquities of the Prize Ring)**

DAVEY GETS IT DONE. Davey Moore captured the Featherweight Championship from Hogan "Kid" Bassey on March 18, 1959 at the Olympic Auditorium by stopping the champ in thirteen rounds. Here, Moore (on the right) again stopped Hogan "Kid" Bassey in a Featherweight Championship bout at the Olympic Auditorium. This time, on August 19, 1959, the bout lasted eleven rounds. Moore next appeared at the Olympic Auditorium on April 8, 1961, in defense of his title and stopped Danny Valdez in one round.

BECERRA. Jose Becerra broke a smile as he displayed a check in the amount of $20,000 for winning the World Bantamweight title. Coming into the July 8, 1959 title fight against Champion Alphonse Halimi, Becerra had a 62-4 mark with two draws and had scored eleven straight knockouts. He knocked out Halimi in eight rounds to capture the crown.

GOOD FIGHTER, TRAGIC END. Curley Lee Chapman (Ocie Lee Chatmon) fought frequently in Hollywood and Los Angeles during the late 1950s. In a short but impressive career, he defeated Johnny Hayden, Paul Andrews and Howard King. But, on October 14, 1959, he was stopped by Cleveland Williams in a bout that ended his ring aspirations. In 1972, Lee drowned his four children and murdered his brother-in-law. He received a life sentence in prison. **(Courtesy Tom Scharf)**

THE BATTLER. Raymundo "Battling" Torres was a crunching puncher with a smashing left hook. During his career, he scored 46 knockouts in 66 bouts. Although he was not a polished boxer, he beat some talented men during his career. On October 15, 1959 at the Olympic Auditorium, he met Johnny Busso, who had victories over Joe Brown and Carlos Ortiz. Here, Torres (on the right) flattens Busso (going down) in two rounds.

JOE PASSES. Joe Levy, 79, a major player in the early days of boxing in the area passed away on December 11, 1959. During his career, Levy was manager of "Mexican" Joe Rivers, matchmaker at the Olympic Auditorium under Jack Doyle and promoted the first boxing card held at Gilmore Stadium.

Levy, Boxing Promoter, Dies

Joe Levy, 79, veteran boxing promoter who staged the first fight at Gilmore Stadium, died yesterday at General Hospital.

Mr. Levy began his career in boxing as the manager of lightweight Joe Rivers, a top rated fighter more than 40 years ago. He later turned to promoting fights and was linked with the top names in boxing in the 20s and 30s.

He leaves a nephew, Eugene Simansky, and a niece, Mrs. Walter Monarch. In recent years he lived at 206 W 6th St.

Services will be held at noon tomorrow in the chapel of Glasband Mortuary. Interment will be in Mount Carmel Cemetery, Bell Gardens.

DOUBLE HEADER. On February 4, 1960, at the Los Angeles Memorial Coliseum, two World Championship bouts were held. To the left is the program for the two title bouts. Jose Becerra successfully defended his Bantamweight crown against Alphonse Halimi in a rematch. This was Becerra's last appearance in Los Angeles. Carlos Ortiz defended his Junior Welterweight title against "Battling" Torres and knocked out the challenger. On February 2, 1961, Ortiz defeated Cisco Andrade at the Olympic Auditorium in a non-title bout. Carlos made his last appearance in the Los Angeles area in 1972 when he won over Greg Potter.

HE WAS A GREAT ONE. Eder Jofre (on the right), rated by many as the best bantamweight ever, captured the NBA Bantamweight title on November 18, 1960 at the Olympic Auditorium when he scored a six round knockout over Eloy Sanchez. During his career, Jofre engaged in 78 bouts and lost only two.

THE CHAMP AND SUGAR FIGHT A DRAW. On December 3, 1960, Middleweight Champion Gene Fullmer (dark trunks) fought a fifteen round draw with the great "Sugar" Ray Robinson at the Sports Arena. Coming into the bout, these two men had a record of 210 bouts with 195 wins, only 12 losses and three draws.

TOUGH BANTAMWEIGHT. Jose Medel (Jose Medel Navarro) was a hard punching Bantamweight Champion of Mexico for more than seven years and a top contender for the world championship during his career. Medel was rated among the top fighters in his weight class for 98 months and the #1 challenger for the title by the NBA in 1961 and 1962. During his career, he defeated such men as Fighting Harada, Walter McGowan, Jesus Pimentel, Jose "Toluco" Lopez, Eloy Sanchez, Dwight Hawkins, Ray Asis, Mitsunori Seki, Herman Marques, Sadao Yaoita, Danny Kid, Ignacio "Zurdo" Pina and Manuel Barrios. Medel made eight appearances in the Los Angeles area. **(Courtesy Antiquities of the Prize Ring)**

Fight 'Boss' Carbo, Four Convicted

Illustrated on Page 3, Part I

Frankie Carbo, long regarded as the boss of boxing in the United States, and four others were convicted Tuesday of extortion.

They were found guilty by a jury of trying to take over control of former welter weight boxing champion Don Jordan by threatening a matchmaker and a man ager.

Leonard Hails Carbo Conviction

Conviction of Frankie Carbo and four others on conspiracy and extortion charges in boxing was hailed Wednesday as a "break" for boxing by Jackie Leonard, former Hollywood fight promoter and key government witness.

Leonard appeared briefly at the Federal Building accompanied by his wife and son and in the company of a U.S. deputy marshal. He had been under guard during the trial.

"This is the best thing that ever happened to boxing," Leonard said. "Although I'm not in it any more, the small promoter and club should get a break."

ORGANIZED CRIME. On May 31, 1961, Frankie Carbo, Frank "Blinky" Palermo, Truman Gibson Jr., Louis Tom Dragna and Joe Sica were convicted of conspiracy and extortion charges in an attempt to take control of the affairs of Don Jordan, former world welterweight champion. Jackie Leonard, former Hollywood boxing promoter, and Donald Nesseth, Jordan's manager, were key witnesses against the convicted. Ernest A. Tolin was the judge of the three month trial. Alvin H. Goldstein, special assistant to U.S. Attorney General, Robert Kennedy, led the prosecution. A jury of ten women and two men found the accused guilty. Said Goldstein, "This is one of the few cases ever tried which reaches to the heart of underworld activities." In December, 1961, U.S. Judge George Boldt sentenced Carbo to 25 years in prison. Sica was sentenced to 20 years while Palermo was given 15 years. Gibson was placed on a five-year probation. In addition, all four men received a $10,000 fine. Dragna's bail was set at $25,000 while Gibson's bail was set at $5,000.

HOLLYWOOD SCRAPPER. Monroe Ratliff had an up-and-down career from the mid-1950s through the early 1960s, but during his fistic career managed to defeat some of the best in the heavyweight division. Ratliff earned victories over such men as Roland LaStarza, Tommy Harrison, Sixto Rodriguez, Reuben Vargas, Alfredo Zuany, Lonnie Malone and Bob Parish.

WORKING HIS WAY UP. Cassius Clay (Muhammad Ali), on the right in this photo, made a big scene in Los Angeles in 1962, scoring knockouts over George Logan on April 23, Alejandro Lavorante on July 20 and Archie Moore on November 15. Seen here, Clay finishes Moore.

BOXING PROMO PASSES. All of his trials, tribulations and "wheelin-n-dealin" ended on April 22, 1962 for Harry "Babe" McCoy when he died of a heart attack. Responsible for developing boxing during the 1940s and 1950s, undergoing a trial for setting up boxing bouts and prohibited from promoting cards in California, "Babe" was a prominent figure in state fisticuffs for nearly twenty years.

Ex-Boxing Promoter McCoy Dies

Heart Attack Fatal to Matchmaker Barred After Probe

Babe McCoy, 62, who ruled boxing here for 15 years until it was shown in 1956 that he was a behind-the-scenes fight-fixer and bosom pal of gangsters, died of a heart attack early Sunday.

TAKING CARE OF BUSINESS. From left to right, Luis Manuel Rodriguez, Aileen Eaton, George Parnassus (seated), Cal Eaton and Raymundo "Battling" Torres are busy making calls and checking out various aspects of the upcoming card in Dodger Stadium on March 21, 1963.

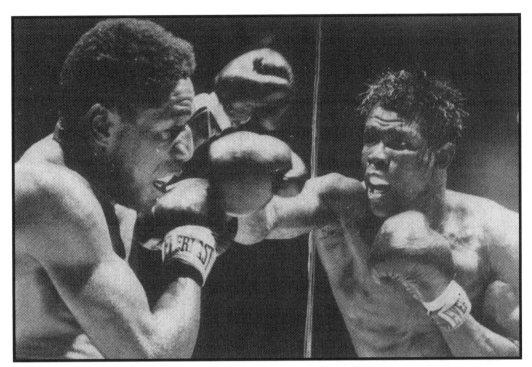

GETTIN' IT ON. Luis Rodriguez (on the left) absorbs a right hander from Emile Griffith but managed to win in fifteen rounds on the March 21, 1963 card at Dodger Stadium to capture the both the WBC and WBA Welterweight Championships of the World. Prior to this bout, on June 3, 1961, Griffith had retained his Welterweight title by stopping Gaspar Ortega in twelve rounds at the Olympic Auditorium.

TRAGIC END TO A GREAT CAREER. Ultiminio "Sugar" Ramos (turning away) won the WBC and WBA Featherweight titles from Davey Moore on the March 21, 1963 card when he defeated the champion in ten rounds at Dodger Stadium. Referee George Latka stopped the bout. Moore went into a coma and died two days later. On the same card, Roberto Cruz knocked out Raymundo "Battling" Torres in one round to win the WBA Junior Welterweight Championship.

AILEEN'S CLUB. The Olympic Boxing Club at 1801 South Grand Avenue in Los Angeles was a busy and prominent place in the boxing activities of Southern California during the 1956 to 1980 years. Mickey Davies came aboard as the matchmaker in 1965. Cal Eaton passed away in 1966 and Aileen Eaton became the sole promoter. Later, Don Chargin was the associate matchmaker and Jimmy Lennon was the announcer.

OLYMPIC BOXING CLUB

1801 So. Grand Ave. • Los Angeles, Calif., 90015 • RI 9-5171

Aileen Eaton	Promoter
Mike Le Bell	General Manager
Mickey Davies	Matchmaker
Don Chargin	Assoc. Matchmaker
Van Barbieri	Publicity
Luis Magana	Publicity, Espanol
Al Santoro	Publicity
Jack Disney	Publicity
Lorraine Chargin	Bldg. Manager
Jimmy Lennon	Announcer
Jack Smith	Timekeeper
Joe Letizia	Box Office

THE CALIFORNIA STATE ATHLETIC COMMISSION
Chairman
Dr. Dan O. Kilrov
Albert C. Diaz, Robert Voight   Douglas Hayden, William K. Houston
Robert Turley, Executive Officer
Clayton Frye, Ass't. Ex. Officer
Roy Tennison, Ass't. Chief Inspector
Ken Gray, Ass't. Chief Inspector
ATHLETIC INSPECTORS (Los Angeles Area)   Larry Zagar and Stewart Mitchell

OUTSTANDING ASSOCIATE AND FUTURE GREAT. Don Chargin (standing) was the associate matchmaker of the super team assembled by Aileen Eaton (seated) at the Olympic Club. Don boxed as a youth and when an injury forced him out of the ring as a competitor, he turned to matchmaker and promoter of bouts. He promoted his first card in 1951 (Eddie Chavez-Manuel Ortiz) and during his career promoted such fights as Carl "Bobo" Olson-Paddy Young, Jerry Quarry-Jimmy Ellis, Joey Giambra-Chico Vejar as well as fighters like Armando "Mando" Ramos, Bobby Chacon, Danny "Little Red" Lopez, Pete Ranzany, Carlos Palomino and Tony Lopez. He was matchmaker at the Olympic Auditorium for many years and head of Don Chargin Productions. Don was inducted to the International Boxing Hall of Fame in 2001.

DOUBLE TROUBLE. Jesus (left) and Jose Luis Pimentel were prominent fighters in the area during the 1960s and into the early 1970s. "Little Poison" as Jesus was called, is rated among the greatest punching bantamweights in ring history. He is a member of the World Boxing Hall of Fame. Jose Luis, a featherweight, had a much shorter career but was a consistent winner. Both men fought for their respective world titles during their careers. **(Courtesy HERALD-EXAMINER COLLECTION / Los Angeles Public Library)**

OH, DANNY BOY. Danny Valdez had a fine nine year career in the ring from 1957 to 1966. During 1958-1959, he lost only one fight – to Dwight Hawkins – while winning twelve. A year after his fight with Hawkins, Danny gained revenge by winning a twelve-rounder against Dwight. In his career, Danny also boasted wins over Ramon "Bobby" Cervantes, Juan Ramirez, Horace "Boots" Monroe, Ricardo Gonzalez, Tony Herrera and Gil Cadilli.

A BUSY CHAMPION. Raul Rojas was a ready, willing and able warrior trained by Jack McCoy. He won the Junior Lightweight Championship (as recognized by the California Boxing Commission) on May 25, 1967 by stopping Vicente Derado in fifteen rounds at the Olympic Auditorium. On September 14, 1967, in defense of his Junior Lightweight title, Rojas defeated Kang Il Suh in fifteen rounds before 9,982 fans. On December 14, 1967, Raul won the Featherweight Championship (as recognized by the state of California) by defeating Antonio Herrera in fifteen rounds and on March 28, 1968, he won the WBA Featherweight Championship by defeating Enrique Higgins in fifteen. The Suh, Herrera and Higgins bouts were held at the Olympic Auditorium.

MAKING IT BIG. Jerry Quarry (on the left) listens to Aileen Eaton, promoter, as Floyd Patterson (standing) speaks to the audience. In just two short years of fighting, Quarry had earned a 23-1 record with three draws. He fought Patterson to a ten round draw on June 9, 1967 at the Memorial Coliseum. Then, in a WBA Heavyweight title elimination bout on October 28 at the Olympic Auditorium, he defeated the former champion in twelve rounds. Jerry next defeated Thad Spencer and gained a title shot at the WBA Champion, Jimmy Ellis. He lost that fight, however.

BY GEORGE. George Parnassus promoted an elimination bout for the Bantamweight Championship at the Inglewood Forum on June 14, 1968. Jesus "Chucho" Castillo toppled Jesus Pimentel in twelve rounds to earn a title shot. A ringside ticket for the press is shown here.

BOXING AT THE FORUM
PRESENTED BY GEORGE PARNASSUS PROMOTIONS

Friday Eve. June 14, 1968 — 8:00 p.m.
12 ROUNDS - WORLD BANTAMWEIGHT ELIMINATION

CHU CHU   JESUS
CASTILLO VS. PIMENTEL

WORKING
PRESS   RETAIN THIS COUPON FOR REFUND
IN CASE CONTEST DOES NOT TAKE

MANDO STEPS UP. Armando "Mando" Ramos (dark trunks) blasts a right to the chin of Hiroshi Kobayashi on his way to a ten round decision victory at the Olympic Auditorium on June 20, 1968. Ramos carried a 21-2 record at this date with 14 knockouts. Next opponent on the list for "Mando" was Lightweight Champion Carlos Teo Cruz, for the WBC and WBA Lightweight titles. "Mando" lost this contest but won a rematch to capture those crowns. Afterwards, he won a couple more world championship bouts in Los Angeles.

A WINNING TEAM. Aileen Eaton, the outstanding and only female boxing promoter in the world as of 1968, is shown with the famous sports announcer, Dick Enberg (center) and matchmaker, Mickey Davies. In a short period of time, Aileen made Los Angeles a center for big fights, week in and week out, and went out of her way to help needy fighters. The talented, wise-cracking Davies was Eaton's matchmaker and ably built up her promotions into top draws. He regularly arranged cards that involved such fighters as Armando "Mando" Ramos, Raul Rojas, Joey Orbillo, Frankie Crawford, Shozo Saijyo and Jerry Quarry.

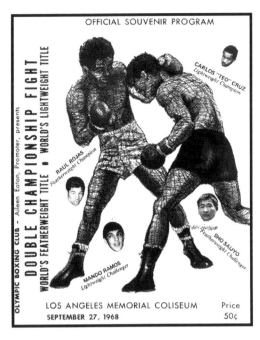

TITLE BOUT DOUBLE HEADER. September 27, 1968 was a big night at the Memorial Coliseum as two World Championship bouts were held there. Carlos Teo Cruz defended his WBC and WBA Lightweight titles against Armando "Mando" Ramos and Raul Rojas took on Shozo Saijyo in defense of his WBA Featherweight title. Both fights lasted the scheduled fifteen rounds. Cruz won a decision but Rojas lost. Shown here is the program for this big event.

GOOD MAN TAKES OVER. Jose Napoles (on the right) stopped Curtis Cokes in thirteen rounds on April 18, 1969 to capture the WBC and WBA Welterweight titles at The Forum in Inglewood. Six months later, on October 17, Napoles defended his crowns against Emile Griffith at The Forum and won a fifteen round decision. It was the twenty-first title fight for Griffith, who engaged in three more before his twenty year career was over. It was the third title fight for Napoles, who went on to fight in 15 more title bouts before he finished his ring career. In all, Napoles engaged in six title contests in Inglewood.

HARD-HITTING BATTLER. On August 22, 1969, Ruben Olivares (walking away) knocked out Lionel Rose in five rounds at the Inglewood Forum to win the WBC and WBA Bantamweight Championships of the World. Ruben was back at The Forum on December 12, 1969 and stopped Alan Rudkin in two rounds to retain his titles. Ruben fought ten world title bouts at The Forum. Olivares is often called the hardest hitting bantamweight of all-time. During his career, he amassed a record of 88-13-3 with 78 knockouts (reports vary).

NEW CHAMP. Here we see Ismael Laguna (sitting) being checked out by a medical doctor while others look on. On March 3, 1970, Laguna stopped Armando "Mando" Ramos in nine rounds to win the WBC and WBA Lightweight Championships at the Sports Arena. Later, he was stripped of his WBC title for allegedly breaking a contract with Aileen Eaton to defend his title in Los Angeles.

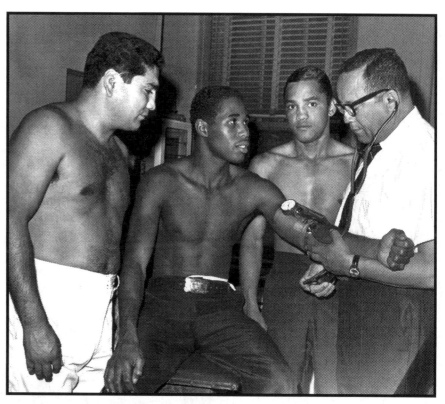

GOLDEN BOXER'S DAY. A special day was declared by Los Angeles Mayor Sam Yorty on August 15, 1970. From left to right are Noble "Kid" Chissell, former Navy Middleweight Champion, professional dancer and actor; Mayor Yorty; and Georgie Levine, welterweight contender.

A HOT ITEM. Ruben Olivares and Jesus "Chucho" Castillo engaged in three highly competitive bouts for the WBC and WBA Bantamweight titles. All were held at the Inglewood Forum. Olivares won the first contest on April 18, 1970 on a fifteen round decision and retained his crowns. Castillo took the second match and captured the titles on October 16, 1970 when Olivares was stopped on cuts in round fourteen. On April 2, 1971, Ruben regained the titles on a fifteen round decision. In all, the two men battled 44 rounds. Shown here is a press ticket to the Olivares-Castillo bout on October 16, 1970.

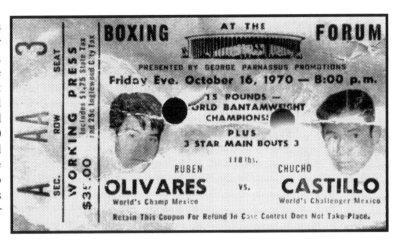

CALIFORNIA BOXING - THEY GOT IT DONE. At George Parnassus' 1971 birthday party were (left to right) Stephen "Suey" Welch (Manager), Tom Gallery (Actor, Promoter, Matchmaker, Television Executive), Kid Mexico (Todd Faulkner; Matchmaker), Parnassus (Manager, Promoter) and Tommy Farmer (Manager)

CAPABLE MAN. Jimmy Robertson was a talented lightweight who fought out of Los Angeles from 1968 to 1974. After losing his first professional fight in June of 1968, he ran off close to 20 straight wins. Following a loss in 1970 to Ruben Navarro, Robertson did not lose again until 1972 against Rodolfo Gonzalez. Jimmy made a game but unsuccessful attempt to take the WBA Lightweight title from Roberto Duran in 1973. When Jimmy was fighting, he had key wins over Manuel Lugo, Beto Maldonado, Al "Scooter" Meza, Jose Luis Cruz, Len Kasey and Ruben Navarro.

A LITTLE PACKAGE OF DYNAMITE. Romeo Anaya (on the left) is shown attacking Enrique Pinder at the Inglewood Forum on August 18, 1973. He knocked out Pinder in three rounds in defense of his WBA Bantamweight crown. Romeo had won the title from Pinder on January 20, 1973 in Panama City, by a third round stoppage. He also had defeated Rogelio Lara in fifteen rounds at the Inglewood Forum on April 28, 1973 to retain his WBA Bantamweight Championship.

GETTIN' EVEN. Muhammad Ali had no idea that Ken Norton was as good as he was when they squared off the first time in March of 1973 and he lost. However, the second time around, Ali was ready and avenged himself. On September 10, 1973 at the Inglewood Forum, he beat Norton in twelve rounds to win back the NABF Heavyweight title. But, the outcome was questionable as 17 of the 21 sportswriters at ringside had Norton the winner on their cards. In the photo to the right, *The Ring* magazine publicized the bout in its September issue.

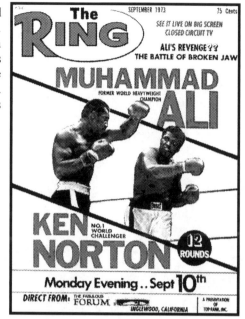

THE CHAMP GETS BELTED. On October 13, 1973 at the Inglewood Forum, Rafael Herrera took on Venice Borkorsor for the WBC Bantamweight Championship. Seen here, Herrera (on the right) gets pounded by a strong left but weathers the storm and goes on to record a fifteen round split-decision win and retain his title. During the years 1967-1986, Herrera fought in Los Angeles, Inglewood, San Diego and San Bernardino on seventeen occasions. **(Courtesy Antiquities of the Prize Ring)**

AN OUTSTANDING CAREER. Armando Muniz was in the ring for nearly nine years and posted a terrific record. During this time, he was the NABF Welterweight Champion and competed for the WBC or WBA Welterweight world titles on four occasions. Armando posted wins over Mike Seyler, Jesus "Chucho" Garcia, "Irish" Gil King, Clyde Gray, Percy Pugh, Adolph Pruitt, Frank Kolovart, Manuel Gonzalez, Ernie Lopez, Dave Oropeza, Hedgemon Lewis, Jimmy Heair and Pete Ranzany.

READY, WILLING, AND ABLE. Rodolfo Gonzalez (on the right) lands a punch while slipping a left hand by Antonio Puddu. Gonzalez stopped Puddu in ten rounds to retain his WBC Lightweight title on October 27, 1973. He had defeated Eubrey "Chango" Carmona in thirteen rounds on November 10, 1972 to win the WBC Lightweight Championship and on March 17, 1973, he beat Ruben Navarro in nine rounds to retain his WBC Lightweight crown. All three of these title bouts were held at the Sports Arena. Nearly six months after this bout with Puddu, Gonzalez lost his title to Guts Ishimatsu.

TAKE THAT. Bobby Chacon (center) smashes Danny "Little Red" Lopez to the ropes during their May 24, 1974 battle at the Sports Arena. Referee John Thomas is about to step in and call a halt to the contest in the ninth round. Over 16,000 fans were in attendance. This was a big win for Chacon who went on to fight for the WBC Featherweight title four months later.

TOUGH OPPONENT. Alfredo Marcano represented a strong obstacle to Bobby Chacon but Bobby won the WBC Featherweight title at the Olympic Auditorium on September 7, 1974 by stopping Marcano in nine rounds. Later, Chacon knocked out Jesus "Papelero" Estrada in two rounds on March 1, 1975 at the Olympic to retain his WBC Featherweight crown.

ROCKY GETS IT DONE. Hollywood continued to show its interest in boxing as Rocky Balboa (Sylvester Stallone), on the left, landed a hook to the jaw of Apollo Creed (Carl Weathers) in one of the exciting *Rocky* movies that brought fans to their feet and stimulated interest in boxing during the late 1970s and early 1980s.

TOP CALIBER MAN. Boasting a 30-2 record over his first five years, Rudy Robles challenged Rodrigo Valdez for the WBC Middleweight title in 1975 but lost a fifteen round decision. Willie Warren, Jorge Rosales, Ron Wilson, David Love, Rudy Cruz, Tony Mundine and Mike Colbert were all counted among Rudy's victims during his career that lasted from 1970-1984.

SPECIAL RECOGNITION. Jacob "Buddy" Baer, left, is given a legislative resolution of commendation by Senator Clare Berryhill, second from the left, during the fall of 1974. Looking on are Gene Garner, second from the right, who fought Baer in 1934, and Ancil Hoffman (far right), who managed both "Buddy" and Max Baer during their careers.

PAUL REVERE PATRIOTS. At the Everett L. Sanders Testimonial Boxing Champions Banquet held at the International Hotel in Los Angeles on October 18, 1974, George Martin (center) presented the *Order of Paul Revere Patriots Award* to Mushy Callahan (left) and Jimmy McLarnin (right).

A GREAT ONE. On November 23, 1974, Alexis Arguello (facing the camera) knocked out Ruben Olivares in thirteen rounds at the Inglewood Forum to win the WBA Featherweight Championship. Arguello knocked out Salvador Torres in three rounds at the Inglewood Forum on June 19, 1976 in defense of his championship and then gave up his title because he had difficulty making the weight limit for title bouts. Fighting a little heavier, Arguello stopped Rey Tam in five rounds on April 29, 1978 at the Forum to retain his WBC Super Featherweight title.

FIVE TITLE BOUTS IN LOS ANGELES FOR CARLOS. Carlos Zarate (on the right) met Rodolfo Martinez at the Inglewood Forum on May 8, 1976 and scored a ninth round knockout to win the WBC Bantamweight Championship. Zarate was back in Inglewood on August 28, 1976 and stopped Paul Ferreri in twelve rounds to retain his title. On October 29, 1977, Carlos knocked out Danilo Batista in six rounds at the Inglewood Forum and on February 25, 1978, he stopped Alberto Davila at the Forum in eight rounds. He was back at the Forum one more time, on March 10, 1979, and flattened Mensah Kpalongo in three rounds. Zarate was inducted into to the International Boxing Hall of Fame in 1994.

LITTLE CHAMP. Guty Espadas (Gustavo Hernan Espadas Cruz) stopped Alfonzo Lopez in thirteen rounds at the Memorial Sports Arena on October 2, 1976 to win the WBA Flyweight Championship of the World. Thirteen months later, on November 19, 1977, Espadas defended his crown and kayoed Alex Santana Guido in eight rounds.

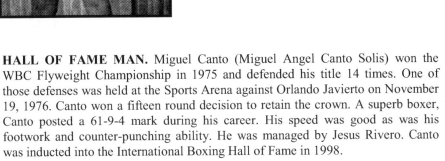

HALL OF FAME MAN. Miguel Canto (Miguel Angel Canto Solis) won the WBC Flyweight Championship in 1975 and defended his title 14 times. One of those defenses was held at the Sports Arena against Orlando Javierto on November 19, 1976. Canto won a fifteen round decision to retain the crown. A superb boxer, Canto posted a 61-9-4 mark during his career. His speed was good as was his footwork and counter-punching ability. He was managed by Jesus Rivero. Canto was inducted into the International Boxing Hall of Fame in 1998.

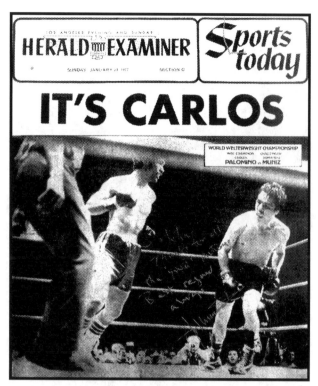

CARLOS IS A WINNER. Carlos Palomino was a popular fighter in the Los Angeles area, having fought here 28 times. Carlos won the WBC Welterweight Championship of the World on June 21, 1976 in London by stopping John Stracey in twelve rounds. On January 22, 1977, he stopped Armando Muniz in fifteen rounds in defense of his title at the Olympic Auditorium. Seen here is coverage by the Los Angeles Herald Examiner that shows Palomino (fighter to the left) about to stop Muniz in the last round to retain his crown. Palomino defended his title again in the "City of Angels" on September 13, 1977 at the Olympic Auditorium and defeated Everaldo Costa Azevedo in fifteen rounds. **(Courtesy Clay Moyle)**

TWO BANTAM CHAMPS HAVE AT IT. When was the last time two unbeaten champions met in a non-title bout? Carlos Zarate (on the left), WBC Bantamweight Champion, and Alfonso Zamora, WBA Bantamweight Champion, met in such a contest at the Inglewood Forum on April 23, 1977. Here, Zamora (on the right) socks Zarate with a hard right but Carlos persisted and stopped Alfonso in round four.

DAN, THE MAN. Danny "Little Red" Lopez (in his boxing gear) holds up the arm of Howie Steindler, owner of the famous Main Street Gym in downtown Los Angeles. On September 13, 1977, Danny stopped Jose Torres in seven rounds in defense of his WBC Featherweight title. Lopez was back in town on April 23, 1978 to defend his WBC Featherweight crown and stopped Jose Francisco DePaula in six rounds. "Little Red" defended his crown again on September 25, 1979 when he stopped Jose Caba in three rounds.

CARLOS WINS AGAIN. On December 10, 1977, Carlos Palomino defended his WBC Welterweight crown against Jose Palacios at the Olympic Auditorium. Palomino won in 13 rounds to retain his title. Then, Carlos defended his crown on May 27, 1978 at the Olympic and defeated Armando Muniz in fifteen rounds. **(Courtesy Antiquities of the Prize Ring)**

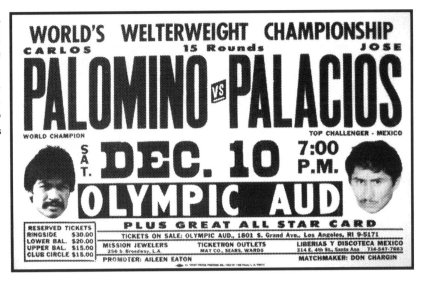

ANOTHER ONE BITES THE DUST. Jose "Pipino" Cuevas (on the right) defeated Harold Weston Jr. in defense of his WBA Welterweight title on March 4, 1978 at the Olympic Auditorium. Cuevas scored a technical knockout after the ninth round. Earlier, Cuevas had knocked out Clyde Gray in two rounds on August 6, 1977 at the Olympic in defense of his WBA Welterweight Championship. He went on to defend his crown three more times in the area, twice at the Inglewood Forum and once at the Sports Arena in Los Angeles with wins over Billy Backus, Scott Clark and Angel Espada.

LADY TYGER. Marian Trimiar, who boxed during 1976-1985, was a pioneer in the sport at a time when boxing by women was quite limited. She aspired to be a boxer when she was a young girl, just ten years of age. The "Lady Tyger" was among the first women to obtain a boxing license in New York state in 1978. She fought exhibition fights before it was legal to box in sanctioned bouts. In her career, Trimiar engaged in 25 contests and won the Women's Lightweight Championship of the World in 1979. Marian appeared at the Olympic Auditorium in 1977 and 1982, winning both fights.

THEY KNEW THEIR STUFF. Bennie Georgino (on the left), manager of Danny "Little Red" Lopez, and Ralph Gambina, who was manager of Cisco Andrade, chat at the Main Street Gym in Los Angeles during the late 1970s. **(Courtesy Clay Moyle)**

Chacon's best is one punch short

By John Beyrooty
Herald Examiner staff writer

"I knew that he had a great punch and that I would have to stay away from him. I knew that he had power to take you out with one shot. I thought I did a good job of staying away from him. But took only one shot."

The man doing the talking was Bobby Chacon and the shot he was referring to came just seconds into the seventh and last round of his fight with Alexis Arguello at the

Schoolboy was absolutely beautiful. Just like the old days.

Feinting, side-stepping, going to the body, getting his punches off first, Chacon had Arguello frustrated. It appeared he was fighting a perfect fight. Until, of course, the uppercut caught up with him.

"I thought I was in control the whole way," said Chacon, who earned $35,000 for last night's effort. "The cut was really the thing that did me in.

"Arguello is a great champion and a great person. But I don't feel

ONE PUNCH SHORT. Displayed above is Herald-Examiner coverage of the Alexis Arguello-Bobby Chacon bout. Arguello (left) defended his WBC Super Featherweight title against Chacon on November 16, 1979 at the Inglewood Forum. Said Bobby, "I knew he had a great punch and that I would have to stay away from him. I knew that he had power to take you out with one shot. I thought I did a good job of staying away from him. But took only one shot." Arguello stopped Chacon in round seven. Arguello was inducted into the International Boxing Hall of Fame in 1992. **(Courtesy Clay Moyle)**

TOP CONTENDER. Jesse Burnett was a battler who had a fine career that bordered on the championship level. From 1972 to early 1977, he posted a 16-3-1 record. Then, he tangled with Miguel Angel Cuello for the WBC Light Heavyweight crown but lost. In 1983, he battled S.T. Gordon for the WBC Cruiserweight crown but was unsuccessful. Burnett also made attempts at the USBA and NABF Light Heavyweight and Cruiserweight titles but never accomplished these goals.

TIME OUT FOR LUNCH. Aileen Eaton, promoter of the Olympic Arena from 1942 until 1980, takes a break for lunch. After doing a wonderful job for nearly forty years, it's time for some rest and relaxation and, maybe, to take in a few fights. At a time when many boxing promoters were going out of business, she ventured to stage boxing cards on a weekly basis. What a magnificent success !

Chapter Seven

The Modern Era

1980-2005

Aileen Eaton "called it a career" in 1980, after being involved in promoting boxing cards at the fabled Olympic Auditorium for nearly forty years. There was still boxing during the 1980s but the era of weekly shows had ended. At the time, there were only two or three clubs that staged weekly cards in the entire country. The number of professional boxing shows presented in the United States on an annual basis was only a fraction of the number held before the days of television.

In 1987, at a reported cost of five million dollars, there was a much-needed effort to refurbish the Olympic Auditorium, sixty-two years after it was built. As a result of the improvements, the seating capacity of the famed arena was a little less than 6,700 and it was a much nicer facility than it was during the 1970s and early 1980s.

Still, there were few boxing cards staged at the Olympic during the next fifteen years. One possible reason was that it was located in a section of Los Angeles that had declined considerably. However, the main reason was that the boxing cards did not generate great interest.

Despite the decreasing number of professional boxing shows at the Olympic Auditorium during the 1980s, the Los Angeles area remained an important site for boxing activity as compared to other parts of the United States. While it was true that the more important bouts of the era took place at either Las Vegas or Atlantic City, there were several venues in the Los Angeles area where boxing cards were held. Notable venues were in Inglewood, Irvine, a city located in nearby Orange County, and Reseda, located in the San Fernando Valley.

From 1979 to early 1981, a promotional organization called Muhammad Ali Professional Sports (MAPS), with Harold "Rossfields" Smith in charge, made a huge impression in the boxing world when it staged a number of large shows featuring many top fighters. The boxing legend, Muhammad Ali, apparently only lent his name to the organization and had little to do with the day-to-day operations.

With a huge amount of money from then-unknown sources, MAPS staged a boxing show at the Santa Monica Civic Auditorium on July 25, 1979. In what became the normal course of events in nearly all of their shows, the gross receipts were far less than the expenditures. Many top fighters fought on MAPS cards during a period of a little less than two years, including Thomas Hearns, Aaron Pryor, Jose "Pipino" Cuevas, Matthew Saad Muhammad, Eddie Mustafa Muhammad and Antonio Cervantes.

In January, 1981, things fell apart at MAPS with the revelation that large amounts of money that financed the boxing cards came from a huge embezzlement operation. Over 21 million dollars was embezzled. As a result, MAPS was shut down.

With the advent of cable television during the 1980s, the number of channels available to people across the United States increased considerably. Area boxing shows on television multiplied and many played to a national audience on ESPN, USA, Fox Sports, HBO and Showtime. Also, there were boxing shows on regional sports cable networks.

Frequent boxing was also presented on the Los Angeles area sports channel called **Prime Ticket**, which later became part of the Fox Sports Network. Many of these shows were staged at the Forum in Inglewood. During the 1980s and 1990s, the Forum often held more boxing shows than the Olympic Auditorium.

During the last two decades of the Twentieth Century, the average attendance at the Forum boxing shows was down by a few thousand. As a result, there were fewer boxing shows at the Forum by the late 1990s.

In the latter part of the 1980s, the major networks showed less boxing than in the 1970s and early 1980s. Consequently, it was difficult for a fighter to become as well known as Muhammad Ali, Roberto Duran or "Sugar" Ray Leonard. However, cable and pay-per-view television generated large amounts of money as compared to previous eras. Also, there was more money available in endorsements than thirty years earlier.

During the 1980s and early 1990s, there were no boxers who drew large crowds in the Los Angeles area like the great local gate attractions of the past. Even one of the greatest of all Mexican boxers, Julio Cesar Chavez, was unable to attract large crowds. However, when he fought at other venues, he drew well. In fact, boxing shows attracted large numbers of Mexican-American and Mexican national fans in such cities as Las Vegas, Sacramento and San Antonio.

At the 1992 Olympics in Barcelona, a young Mexican-American from East Los Angeles named Oscar De La Hoya won a gold medal, capping a brilliant amateur career. As a professional, De La Hoya became the most popular non-heavyweight boxer in the world. In addition to winning world titles in weight classes ranging from super featherweight to light middleweight, Oscar earned far more money than any other Latino boxer in history.

Another area boxer who parlayed a brilliant amateur career into a sparkling career in the professional ranks was "Sugar" Shane Mosley, who went on to win world championships in the lightweight, welterweight and light middleweight divisions. Like many other Los Angeles-based boxers of the 1980s and 1990s, both De La Hoya and Mosley had most of their major bouts in other cities.

The construction of a new large indoor arena called the Staples Center in Downtown Los Angeles signaled a new era in sports in the area. The Staples Center became the home arena for two Los Angeles teams of the National Basketball Association, the Lakers and the Clippers, and a team of the National Hockey League, the Kings. Still, Las Vegas and Atlantic City continued to be the most important venues for major boxing events. However, there were a few important bouts at the Staples Center.

The first bout between "Sugar" Shane Mosley and Oscar De La Hoya took place in June of 2000 before a large crowd at the Staples Center and drew the first million-dollar gate for a professional boxing card in California. Mosley won a split decision in this contest. As a result of this victory, many regarded Mosley as the best "pound-for-pound" boxer in the world until he lost two bouts to Vernon Forrest. Then, Mosley turned things around when he won for a second time over De La Hoya in a rematch staged in Las Vegas.

In 2003, there was a World Heavyweight Championship bout between Lennox Lewis, the champion, and challenger Vitali Klitschko, at the Staples Center. It was the first World Heavyweight title bout since the late 1950s when Floyd Patterson successfully defended his title against Roy "Cut-and-Shoot" Harris at Wrigley Field. Klitschko gave Lewis a very rough time in an exciting bout. However, Klitschko sustained a vicious cut on the left eyelid and the bout was stopped in the sixth round and Lewis retained his title.

Then, Lewis retired and in 2004, Klitschko and Corrie Sanders fought for the World Boxing Council version of the title at the Staples Center. Although he experienced some rough moments, Klitschko stopped the crude but hard-punching southpaw from South Africa.

For the first time since being refurbished in 1987, the Olympic Auditorium hosted a capacity crowd at a boxing show when the very popular Fernando Vargas appeared in 2003. Around this time, the popular De La Hoya ventured into promoting fights and his Golden Boy Boxing Promotions staged boxing cards in a number of cities with a large Latino population.

Despite having some rocky moments, Los Angeles has remained active in boxing to this day. With a long, colorful boxing history and a large fan base, it appears that the huge metropolis is destined to host many professional boxing cards, both large and small, in the foreseeable future.

LUPE, LUPE. "Lupe" Pintor (Jose Guadalupe Pintor Guzman, standing) defended his WBC Bantamweight title twice in the Los Angeles area in 1980. Early in the year, on February 9 at the Inglewood Forum, he stopped Alberto Sandoval in twelve rounds to retain his crown. Then, on September 19 at the Olympic Auditorium, he knocked out Johnny Owen in the twelfth round. Owen was a promising young fighter who carried a sterling 25-1-1 record into the bout. Unfortunately, he died on November 4 as the result of injuries sustained in the bout.

THREE BALTAZARS FROM LOS ANGELES. In the photo below, "Dad" Baltazar (center) stands between Frankie (to our left) and Tony (to our right). "Dad" taught his sons how to box and worked with them from the time they were toddlers. He worked the corners during their bouts too. A third son, Bobby, also boxed.

A FINE FIGHTER. Frankie was a Super Featherweight who fought here often during 1976-1991. He built an impressive 28-1-1 record that earned him a NABF (North American Boxing Federation) Super Featherweight title shot at Rafael

"Bazooka" Limon on July 24, 1980 at the Olympic Auditorium. Limon won on a fourth round stoppage. Afterwards, Frankie ran off ten more wins before losing an eight round decision to Eloy Montano in Las Vegas in 1989

TONY THE TIGER. Tony had a wonderful career that began in 1979. Up through 1985, he had a 26-2-1 record, losing only to Howard Davis Jr. and Robin Blake. After a break of nearly three years, he returned and racked up a number of wins through late 1990, including victories over Miguel Angel Dominguez and Pedro Laza. In August of 1990, he lost a WBO Light Welterweight title fight against Hector "Macho" Camacho. Another unsuccessful attempt to win that crown came against Carlos Gonzalez in 1993.

EDDIE AIN'T EASY. Eddie Mustafa Muhammad (Edward Lee Gregory) is shown here on the right with Aaron Pryor and his son. At the Olympic Auditorium on November 28, 1980, Eddie stopped Rudi Koopmans in three rounds to retain his WBA Light Heavyweight Championship.

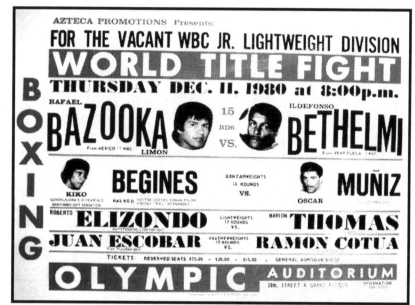

THE BAZOOKA. On December 11, 1980, at the Olympic Auditorium, Rafael "Bazooka" Limon stopped Ildefonso Bethelmi in fifteen rounds to win the WBC Super Featherweight crown (called Junior Lightweight on the poster). Limon was back at the Olympic on September 18, 1982 and stopped Chung-Il Choi in seven rounds in defense of his WBC Super Featherweight Championship. **(Courtesy Antiquities of the Prize Ring)**

CHAVA! Salvador "Chava" Sanchez (left) attacks Nicky Perez on July 11, 1981 en route to a ten round decision victory. Tragically, a little over a year later, Sanchez was killed in an automobile accident. In a brilliant career that lasted from 1975 to 1982, Salvador posted a 44-1-1 record with wins over such opponents as Hector Cortez, James Martinez, Richard Rozelle, Danny "Little Red" Lopez, Ruben Castillo, Patrick Ford, Juan LaPorte, Roberto Castanon, Wilfredo Gomez, Jorge Garcia and Azumah Nelson. **(Courtesy HERALD-EXAMINER COLLECTION / Los Angeles Public Library)**

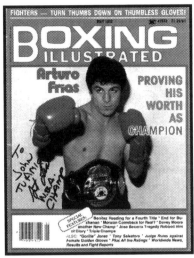

FRIAS THE WINNER. At the Olympic Auditorium, on January 30, 1982, Arturo Frias retained his WBA Lightweight title when he won a "Technical Decision" against Ernesto Espana in nine rounds. His nice 24-1 career record and two title defenses earned him the cover of the May 1982 Boxing Illustrated magazine. **(Courtesy Clay Moyle)**

AN ALL-TIME GREAT GETS INDUCTED. In the photo to the right, Sandy Saddler (on the left) was inducted into the World Boxing Hall of Fame in 1982. Here, he is shown receiving the award. Saddler fought for thirteen years, posted a 145-16-2 record, including 103 knockouts, and won the World Junior Lightweight and Featherweight Championships. He is most famous for his wars with Willie Pep in '48, '49, '50 and '51.

ADRIANO ARREOLA. A good fighter, Arreola won nine of his first eleven bouts during 1980-1981. Then, he went on a 24 of 30 tear from 1982-1986, prior to fighting Johnny De La Rosa in a losing cause for the WBC Continental Americas Super Featherweight title. A couple of contests later, Adrian battled Irving Mitchell for the Featherweight Championship of California, but lost. In 1992, at the end of his career, Arreola once more competed for the WBC Continental Americas Super Featherweight crown but fell short against Frank Avelar. During his career, Arreola had victories over such men as Sergio Castro, John Feeney, Mark Davis, Steve Romero, Jimmy Jackson, Felix Rodriguez and "Lupe" Pintor.

GREAT ONES HAVE AT IT. Two big names of the ring, Roberto Duran (on the left) and "Pipino" Cuevas (right), tangled at the Sports Arena on January 29, 1983. Duran, who had manhandled the lightweight division ever since 1968, had moved up in weight in 1978. Mr. "Hands of Stone" had lost only four fights in 79 contests but three of them had occurred since 1980. Cuevas, a great welterweight champion from 1976 to 1980 was on the downgrade. Each man had a tremendous following in the area. The fight was the talk of the town. The atmosphere was thick and tense. The issue was settled in the fourth round with Duran the winner.

A SUPER FIGHTER. Julio Cesar Chavez, one of the best fighters of all time, fought in the Los Angeles area on nine occasions, three times for a world championship. During a remarkable career, Julio posted a 108-6-2 record. His first appearance here was at the Olympic Auditorium against Romero Sandoval on June 15, 1983, when he scored a three round knockout. His last appearance here was at the Staples Center on May 28, 2005 when he won a ten round decision against Ivan Robinson.

NOTHING LIKE A GOOD DINNER WITH FRIENDS. In the above photo, Alexis Arguello, second from the right, who fought in Inglewood several times during his career, takes dinner with Bob Armstrong, on the right. Phil Silvers and his lady are on the left.

EXPLOSIVE. On June 15, 1983, at the Olympic Auditorium, Jaime Garza (walking away) stopped Bobby Berna in the second round to capture the vacant WBC Super Bantamweight Championship. Garza defended his title once and then lost it to Juan "Kid" Meza. Berna bounced back from the defeat to win the IBF Super Bantamweight crown against Seung Il Suh but subsequently lost it back to him.

HIGHLY RANKED. Lilly Rodriguez was a versatile featherweight in women's boxing in the 1970s and early 1980s. She came from a famous family that pioneered kickboxing and was the sister of then world champion kickboxer Benny "The Jet" Urquidez. During her career, Lilly fought such greats as Lucia Rijker (in kickboxing), Marian "Lady Tyger" Trimiar, and the World Featherweight Champion, Toni Lear Rodriguez, whom she defeated. Lilly fought on the All-Women boxing card in California on July 13, 1979. She also fought at Madison Square Garden and the Olympic Auditorium, where she appeared on cards with a number of famous boxers. Lilly was ranked as the #2 Woman Featherweight during 1981-1983 and #3 during 1984. **(Courtesy HERALD-EXAMINER COLLECTION / Los Angeles Public Library)**

CALIFORNIA CHAMP. Felipe Canela (on the left) is shown with his trainer, Larry Soto. Canela waged ring wars from 1980-1988 and had earned a 20-1-1 mark going into his March 30, 1984 bout with Nino LaRocca. Felipe won the Welterweight Championship of California on two occasions, 1983 and 1986. During his fine career, he defeated such fighters as Jerry Cheatham, Hedgemon Robertson, Alphonso Long, Richard Aguirre, "Young" Dick Tiger, Roman George and Derwin Richards.

THE BRAIN AND HIS TEAM. Below right, Manager Bennie Georgino (in the center) stands between Alberto Davila (to our left) and Jaime Garza (to our far right), two world champions. Trainer Johnny Montes is behind Georgino. Garza, a wonderful hitter and active fighter in Los Angeles, captured the vacant WBC Super Bantamweight Championship during his career. Davila appeared many times in Los Angeles. He attempted to win a World Bantamweight title three times without success. But, on September 1, 1983 at the Olympic Auditorium, Albert knocked out Francisco "Kiko" Bejines in twelve rounds to capture the WBC Bantamweight crown. He was inducted into the World Boxing Hall of Fame in 1997.

RAW DEAL. Above left, in the 23rd Olympiad Boxing bouts on August 5, 1984 at the Sports Arena, the United States boxing team won eight Gold Medals. However, Evander Holyfield (right) was disqualified for hitting after the bell. Holyfield became known as the "Real Deal" and went on to win the Cruiserweight and Heavyweight Championships of the World and rank as an All-Time great. **(Courtesy HERALD-EXAMINER COLLECTION / Los Angeles Public Library)**

KING MEZA. On April 19, 1985, Dr. Jerry Buss and Don King co-promoted world title bouts at the Inglewood Forum. Juan "Kid" Meza, who had knocked out Jaime Garza to win the WBC Super Bantamweight title, successfully defended his crown against Mike Ayala with a sixth round stoppage. On the same card, Julio Cesar Chavez stopped Ruben Castillo to retain his WBC Super Featherweight crown. Meza, who built a 45-9 record with 37 knockouts from 1977-1997, was managed by Jimmy Montoya. He fought in the area on twelve occasions.

TALENT ON PARADE. Here is a poster image for the February 3, 1987 bout at the Inglewood Forum between Frankie Duarte and Bernardo Pinango. Duarte, the challenger with 50 bouts of experience attempted to remove the WBA Bantamweight crown from the head of Pinango, who possessed a 20-2-2 record. After battling fifteen rounds, the champion Pinango gained the decision and kept his title. In June of 1987, on national television, Duarte stopped Alberto Davila in a ten round bloody battle for the NABF Bantamweight title. **(Courtesy Antiquities of the Prize Ring)**

SLICK IN THE RING, SLICK OUT. WBC Featherweight Champion Azumah Nelson retained his title when he won a twelve round decision over Marcos Villasana on February 25, 1986 at the Inglewood Forum. Nelson repeated his performance against Villasana on August 29, 1987 at the Olympic Auditorium by winning a twelve rounder for the crown. The following January, Nelson relinquished the title to fight as a Super Featherweight. On February 29, 1988, Nelson defeated Mario Martinez in an unpopular decision of twelve rounds to capture the vacant WBC Super Featherweight title at the Inglewood Forum. After an absence from California of more than seven years, Nelson appeared in Indio during 1995 and stopped Gabriel Ruelas in five rounds to retain his WBC Super Featherweight crown

THE BLACK MAMBA. Roger Mayweather appeared in the area on eleven occasions during his career. On November 12, 1987, he stopped Rene Arredondo in six rounds at the Sports Arena to capture the WBC Light Welterweight title. He defended his crown twice at the Sports Arena during 1988 with wins over Mauricio Aceves and Rodolfo "Gato" Gonzalez. Roger lost the crown to Julio Cesar Chavez in 1989 at the Inglewood Forum. He appeared three more times in the area during 1992.

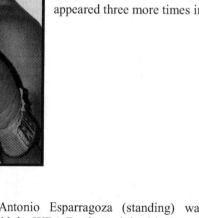

A CAPABLE CHAMPION. Antonio Esparragoza (standing) was an explosive right hand hitter who held the WBA Featherweight title from 1987-1991. During his career, he knocked out 75 percent of his foes and defeated such men as Johnny De La Rosa, Steve Cruz, Pascual Aranda, Jean-Marc Renard and Mitsuru Sugiya. On June 23, 1988, Antonio fought a twelve round draw with Marcos Villasana at the Sports Arena and retained his crown.

SECOND TO NOBODY. Michael Nunn fought in and around Reseda and Inglewood frequently during his early years, 1984-1987. He won the California Middleweight title in 1986 and on July 28, 1988, he proved what he had been saying all along – that he was "Second To None" when he won the IBF Middleweight World Championship by stopping Frank Tate in nine rounds in Las Vegas.

BIG NIGHT. Here, at the World Boxing Hall of Fame Banquet in October of 1988, are (left to right) Charlie Casas, Jake LaMotta (holding a cigar), Jimmy Lennon Sr. and Stu Mitchell at the podium.

TITLE FIGHT. Julio Cesar Chavez captured the WBC Light Welterweight from Roger Mayweather on May 13, 1989 at the Great Western Forum when he stopped the defending champ in ten rounds. The bout was promoted by Don King and witnessed by 10,052 fans.

THERE HE GOES. Jorge "Maromero" Paez was a crowd pleaser from 1984 until 2003, fighting in the area on 16 cards and winning on all but two. His first bout here was on October 23, 1989 against Allan Makitoki and his last on September 28, 2002 when he met Juan Angel Macias. Both were victories. One of his losses took place on November 6, 1992 when he battled Rafael Ruelas for the NABF Lightweight crown at the Inglewood Forum. Another defeat was at the hands of Genaro Hernandez at the Arrowhead Pond in 1995. Paez successfully defended his WBC Continental Americas Super Featherweight title at the Forum in 1997 against Julian Wheeler.

JULIO AND HIS BUDDIES. Julio Cesar Chavez (center) is shown with movie actors Jimmy Smits (left) and Ricardo Montalban (right). All three guys are handsome fellows but the one in the middle has a banged up eye.

PEDRO BECOMES CHAMP. On November 5, 1990, Pedro Decima stopped Paul Banke in four rounds at the Inglewood Forum to win the WBC Super Bantamweight Championship. This was his only appearance in California. He lost the title to Kiyoshi Hatanaka in his very next bout. During his career, he posted a fine 31-4 record with 21 knockouts.

A VICTORY FOR VICTOR. Victor Rabanales (right) tosses a right at Chang-Kyun Oh during the July 27, 1992 WBC Interim Bantamweight title fight at the Forum. Rabanales appeared at the Forum nine times during 1990-1993, including four title contests. He scored eight wins and lost only to Greg Richardson.

A WONDERFUL CROWD FAVORITE. Jimmy Lennon Sr. (James Frederick Lennon Sr.), on the right, is shown with his son, Jimmy Lennon Jr. at a gathering. Jimmy was the "Golden Voice of Southland Boxing" for more than 40 years and was always enjoyed by the fans for his honesty, charisma, personality, talent and energy. His fluent Spanish was a treat for the Hispanic fans, too. In addition to being an exceptional and entertaining announcer, Jimmy also sang the National Anthem. Son Jimmy Jr. is coming along well in his own right as a talented ring announcer.

A FREQUENT FIGHTER. Humberto "Chiquita" Gonzalez (right) is shown knocking out Napa Kiatwanchai on September 14, 1992. "Chiquita" fought for eight world title bouts at the Inglewood Forum. Another was held at the Arrowhead Pond in Anaheim. During a magnificent career, Gonzalez posted a 43-3 record with 31 knockouts. His first appearance in Inglewood occurred on June 4, 1990 against Luis Monzote and resulted in a technical knockout victory. He appeared for the last time on July 15, 1995 against Saman Sorjaturong.

NORM AND TONY. Tony DeMarco (left) and Norm Crosby meet at the 1993 World Boxing Hall of Fame "Gathering of Champions" in Los Angeles. **(Courtesy Clay Moyle)**

A VERY ACTIVE PLACE. Here is a photo of the Great Western Forum in Inglewood. Many championship contests have been held here. Its programs represent the very best in boxing. Everyone associated with the Forum does a wonderful job.

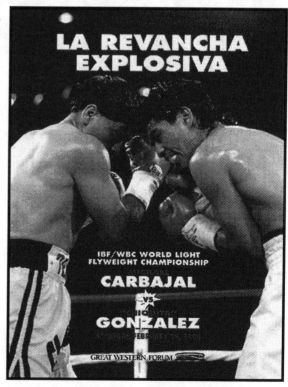

TWO GOOD MEN. On February 19, 1994, at the Great Western Forum, two good men had a fight. One had to win, one had to lose. Humberto "Chiquita" Gonzalez, 38-2, won while Michael Carbajal, 30-0, lost. A split decision winner in twelve rounds, Gonzalez captured the WBC and IBF Light Flyweight titles. Carbajal had won against him earlier in 1993. The two outstanding fighters met once more, on November 12, 1994, and Gonzalez came out the victor again.

MOVIE ACTOR OR FIGHTER? On the March 5, 1994 card at the Olympic Auditorium, handsome Oscar De La Hoya stopped Jimmy Bredahl in ten rounds to win the WBO Super Featherweight Championship of the World. Then, on December 10, 1994, De La Hoya stopped John Avila in nine rounds, also at the Olympic, to retain his WBO Lightweight crown.

GABRIEL. Gabriel Ruelas (right) won the NABF Super Featherweight title, WBC Super Featherweight crown and the IBA Intercontinental Lightweight Championship. In a fine career, he won 49 contests and lost just seven. During his tenure in the ring, Gabriel defeated such men as Aaron Lopez, Alvaro Bohorquez, Tomas Valdez, Ditau Paul Molefyane, Mike Grow, Jesse James Leija, Freddie Libertore, Jimmy Garcia and James Crayton. Brother Rafael was also a top boxer. Winner of many titles, beginning with the Featherweight Championship of California, Rafael Ruelas went on to capture the NABF Featherweight crown, NABF Lightweight crown and the IBF Lightweight Championship. In a wonderful career that saw him win 53 bouts and lose only 4, Rafael defeated such men as Steve Cruz, Rocky Lockridge, Jorge Paez, Darryl Tyson, Freddie Pendleton and Livingstone Bramble.

GOSPEL ACCORDING TO KING JAMES. On March 5, 1994, James "Lights Out" Toney stopped Tim Littles in four rounds at the Olympic Auditorium to win the IBF Super Middleweight title. Shown here, Toney raises his hand in victory. By his side is his pretty manager, Jackie Kallen. Toney went on to capture titles in the Light Heavyweight, Cruiserweight, and Heavyweight divisions, although the WBA Heavyweight crown was denied to him due to substance testing.

A SUDDEN END. Verno Phillips (arms raised) stopped Jaime Llanes in seven rounds at the Inglewood Forum on July 25, 1994 to win the WBO Light Middleweight Championship.

HARD HITTER. On February 20, 1995 at the Inglewood Forum, Sammy Fuentes (on the right) stopped Fidel Avendano in two rounds to win the WBO Light Welterweight title

HEY HOMBRE, TAKE THAT. Carlos Alberto Hernandez (right) throws a punch at Ramon Sanchez in their April 10, 1995 bout at the Forum. Hernandez scored a knockout in the fourth round. During his career, Carlos appeared in the area 29 times and posted 26 victories against a two losses and a draw.

HAVING FUN. Fabela Chavez, scrappy featherweight of the 1945-1955 years, gives a grin at the World Boxing Hall of Fame 16th Annual Banquet of Champions in Los Angeles on October 14, 1995. We lost Fabela in 2003.

THREE MUSKETEERS. Don Fraser (center) served as a promoter, matchmaker, manager, publicist, writer, executive and corner man in a long career dedicated to boxing. Don stands between Rafael "Bazooka" Limon (on the left) and Bobby Chacon (on the right) at a get together in 1996. Limon and Chacon had a great ring rivalry during their careers. Both Fraser and Chacon were inducted into the International Boxing Hall of Fame in 2005.

THE NOW PLACE. The Staples Center opened in 1999 and has been a popular site for providing the area with the very best in entertainment for sports and other types of activities. There have been a number of World Championship bouts held here and many outstanding boxers such as "Sugar" Shane Mosley, Erik Morales, Roy Jones Jr., Lennox Lewis, Rafael Marquez, Daniel Reyes, Vitali Klitschko, Glen Johnson and Bernard Hopkins have been victorious in these fights. **(Photo Provided By Jan Sanders, Los Angeles, Ca)**

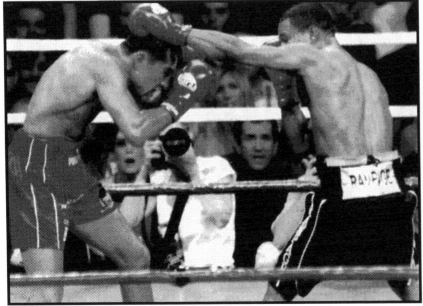

SUGAR BEATS THE GOLDEN BOY. On June 17, 2000 at the Staples Center, "Sugar" Shane Mosley (on the right) defeated Oscar De La Hoya in twelve rounds in a bout for the WBC and IBA Welterweight titles. This was only De La Hoya's second career loss, the first being a questionable 12 round decision to Felix "Tito" Trinidad in 1999. A few fights after this, Mosley suffered two losses to Vernon Forrest. Later, another win against De La Hoya restored his reputation.

POUND FOR POUND, THE BEST AROUND! A triple header of world title bouts was held at the Staples Center on July 28, 2001. Roy Jones Jr. (to the right) defended his numerous Light Heavyweight Championships against Julio Gonzalez and won a decision in twelve rounds to retain his titles. On the same card, Erik Morales retained his WBC Featherweight title by winning a twelve round decision against In Jin Chi. In a third title match, Andrew Lewis kept his WBA Welterweight crown when he accidentally butted heads with Ricardo Mayorga in the second round and the contest was halted.

TOUGHER THAN EXPECTED. On June 21, 2003, Lennox Lewis (on the left) defended his WBC and IBO Heavyweight titles against Vitali Klitschko at the Staples Center. It was the first Heavyweight Championship held in Los Angeles since Floyd Patterson met Roy Harris in 1958. This time, Lewis, usually taller than his foes at 6'5", was in against a man nearly six feet eight inches tall. He found it awkward and tough going. Early in the battle, Klitschko landed a number of stiff left jabs to Lewis' head. He also stung the champion with several hard overhand rights. In round two, it appeared that Lewis was ready to go. But, he hung on. Klitschko sustained a terrible gash over his left eye early in the contest. This, a cut under the eye, and a split lip led the ringside physician to finally stop the contest following round six. Lewis won by stoppage and retained his titles. **(Photo Provided By Tom Hogan/HoganPhotos)**

TWICE THE TALENT. The ring is crowded and Vitali Klitschko (to the far right) is standing on the ropes raising his hand in victory. On April 24, 2004 at the Staples Center before 17,320 fans, Klitschko battled Corrie Sanders for the vacant WBC Heavyweight title. In an old fashioned battle of experienced, heavy hitting big men, Vitali stopped Corrie in round eight to claim the crown and avenge his brother's earlier loss to Sanders. **(Photo Provided By Jan Sanders, Los Angeles, Ca)**

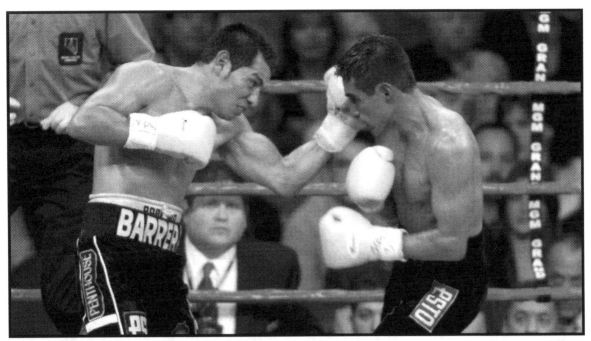

TWO GREAT ONES TANGLE. Shown here, Marco Antonio Barrera (left) and Erik Morales (right) go toe to toe in one of their contests. These two outstanding fighters performed in the area on several occasions. Morales defeated Barerra in a split decision in February of 2000. Then, in June of 2002, Barrera won over Morales, handing Erik his first loss in 42 bouts. In a rubber match in November of 2004, Barrera won a decision in a close battle. **(Photo Provided By Tom Hogan/HoganPhotos)**

A MAN OF DESTINY. Glen Johnson takes a ride on the shoulders of his cornermen following his victory over Antonio Tarver at the Staples Center on December 18, 2004 to win the IBO Light Heavyweight Championship. Tarver, who was involved in a questionable decision that went against him when he met Roy Jones Jr. in their first bout, came out on the short end of a decision against Johnson. The champion bore in on Antonio throughout the fight and apparently impressed the judges enough to gain the win. At times during the contest, it appeared that Tarver may have outboxed his man enough to win. **(Photo Provided By Jan Sanders, Los Angeles, Ca)**

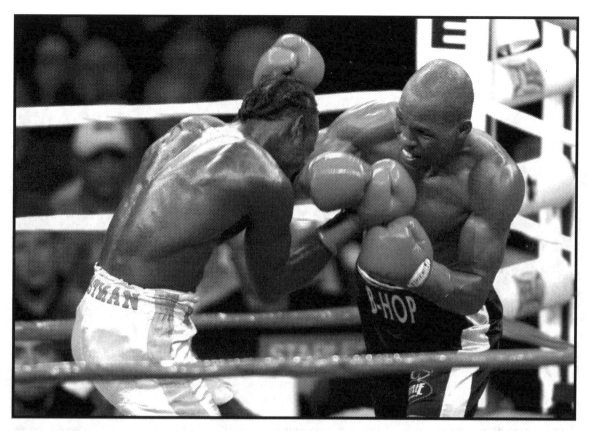

THE EXECUTIONER. Bernard Hopkins (right) tangled with Howard Eastman (left), who boasted a 40-1 record, on February 19, 2005 at the Staples Center with his Middleweight championships at stake. As it turned out, the risk was not that great. Hopkins counter-punched and methodically peppered Eastman with telling blows and won the decision in twelve rounds. At this point in his career, the forty year old Hopkins had fought his way to a 46-2-1 mark with losses only to Clinton Mitchell, in his first professional bout, and Roy Jones Jr. He had gone nearly 12 years without a defeat and had defended his titles 20 times. This was the first Middleweight title fight in Los Angeles since Gene Fullmer and "Sugar" Ray Robinson battled to a draw in 1960. **(Photo Provided By Tom Hogan/HoganPhotos)**

SOME KIND OF TALENT. Unbeaten Lucia Rijker, the 5'6" "Lady Tyson," also labeled as the "Dutch Destroyer," began her career in March, 1996 with a knockout win in Los Angeles. In November, 1997, she won her ninth victory, fighting at the Olympic Auditorium, and in June, 2003 at the Staples Center, gained her sixteenth win. Along the way, in 1998, Lucia captured the Women's Light Welterweight Championship of the World, which she holds today. A former kickboxing world champion who never lost, Rijker appeared in the recent Warner Brothers motion picture, *Million Dollar Baby*, that starred Clint Eastwood, Morgan Freeman and Hilary Swank. Lucia also assisted in the training of actress Swank during the making of the film. **(Photo Provided By Tom Hogan/HoganPhotos)**

About The Authors

Tracy Callis has been researching boxing history and the records of boxers for 45 years and has produced rare, updated records for many boxers. He possesses an outstanding knowledge of boxing history and has a strong interest in boxers of all weight classes from every historical period.

Callis is the Director of Historical Research for *The Cyber Boxing Zone (www.cyberboxingzone.com)* internet website and an Elector for the *International Boxing Hall of Fame*. He is also a member of the *International Boxing Research Organization (IBRO)* and a contributor to the *British Boxing Board of Control Yearbook*.

In the past, he was a contributing editor to the *Ring Record Book* for a number of years and a member of the *World Boxing Historians Association (WBHA)*. In 2002, Tracy co-authored the book, *Philadelphia's Boxing Heritage 1876-1976,* and was a historical consultant on the Jim Jeffries book, *A Man Among Men*.

In his capacity for *The Cyber Boxing Zone*, Tracy is the lead researcher and historian. The site has **350,000-400,000** viewers per month. He researches data, updates boxing records and writes articles for this site.

Charles E. "Chuck" Johnston developed a strong interest in boxing and its history when Muhammad Ali made his storied comeback during the early 1970s. While attending the University of California at Santa Barbara in the middle 1970s, Chuck became interested in doing research on the history of boxing with a great emphasis on his home state of California. He would go on to find unrecorded bouts of numerous boxers who were active from 1880 to 1945.

Chuck is a member of *the **International Boxing Research Organization (IBRO)*** and an editor on the *Boxing Records* internet website (*www.boxrec.com*). In the past, he was a contributing editor to the *Ring Record Book* for a number of years and a historical consultant on the Jack Johnson biography, *Unforgivable Blackness, The Rise and Fall of Jack Johnson*, by Geoffrey C. Ward.